S0-BEH-436

U2

THE EARLY DAYS

A Delta Book
Published by
Dell Publishing
a division of
Bantam Doubleday Dell Publishing Group, Inc.
666 Fifth Avenue,
New York, New York 10103

This work first published in Great Britain by Mandarin Paperbacks,
an imprint of the Octopus Publishing Group.

Text Copyright © 1989 Bill Graham
Illustrations copyright © 1989 Patrick Brocklebank,
James Mahon and Hugo McGuinness.

All rights reserved. No part of this book may be reproduced or
transmitted in any form or by any means, electronic or mechanical,
including photocopying, recording or by any information storage and
retrieval system, without the written permission of the Publisher,
except where permitted by law.

The trademark Delta ® is registered in the U.S. Patent and
Trademark Office.

Library of Congress Cataloging-in-Publication Data
Graham, Bill.
U2, the early days/text Bill Graham; photographs by
Patrick Brocklebank, James Mahon, Hugo McGuinness;
edited by Amy Garvey.

p.   cm.
ISBN 0-385-30081-6
1. U2 (Musical group). 2. Rock musicians – Ireland – Biography.
I Garvey, Amy, II. Title.
ML421.U2G7 1990   89 – 25990
782.42166'092'2–dc20   CIP
(B)

Printed in the United States of America
First U.S.A. printing
May 1990
10 9 8 7 6 5 4 3 2 1

U2

THE EARLY DAYS

TEXT BY
BILL GRAHAM
PHOTOGRAPHS BY
PATRICK BROCKLEBANK
JAMES MAHON
HUGO McGUINNESS
DESIGN BY
STEVE AVERILL
EDITED BY
AMY GARVEY

Delta

Bill Graham is a founding member of Dublin's *Hot Press* and the first writer to champion U2, introducing them to Paul McGuinness, who became their manager. He shares a birthday with another Mandarin author, Michael Jackson.

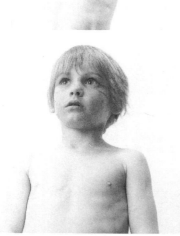

Patrick Brocklebank was a photographer for *Hot Press* and *In Dublin* magazine in the late seventies. From 1979 to 1988 he was a graphic designer for *In Dublin.* He is now a freelance graphic artist.

James Mahon is a childhood friend of Bono. During 1978 and 1979 he worked as a freelance photographer for *Hot Press*, while studying engineering at Trinity College Dublin. He is now working towards his Ph.D in computer science.

Hugo McGuinness studied graphic design at the Dun Laoghaire School of Art in the late seventies. Simultaneously, he began work as a freelance photographer, contributing to numerous magazines in Ireland and abroad. In 1982 he moved to Scandinavia and then returned to Ireland in 1988, where he now works as both a photographer and music publicist.

PREFACE

U2: The Early Days is not a full-scale biography of U2's early Dublin career. Instead it's intended as a biographical sketch in words and pictures, based on the memories and impressions of those who saw U2 growing up as a band in Dublin.

Because photographs involve detachment, the text is as much about how U2 were perceived. The views aren't only from the angle of their allies because U2 also encountered the apathetic and the antagonistic. It would be entirely wrong to believe U2 cruised effortlessly towards their destiny.

Photographs can also be more reliable than memories, ten years after. My witnesses couldn't always be guaranteed to get it right. One good friend, refusing to be interviewed, blurted out: 'I can't remember a thing, Bill. I was drunk all the time.' Certainly there were moments, researching this book and weighing the contradictory stories, when I suspected she had spoken the wisest words. Still I persisted. At the least, I believed that the Irish musical context of the early U2 needed to be explained.

But my text involves hindsight; the photographs of Patrick Brocklebank, Hugo McGuinness and James Mahon don't. Sometimes these pictures show U2 goofing off. Or playing with early image ideas that sometimes succeeded but equally often didn't. But mostly, they show them as U2, a live band in early innocent awe, not so much of themselves, as of the experience and power of rock itself.

And I think all four of us, and Steve Averill equally, were in awe of that power. We really didn't believe a young Dublin band could be so inspirational. Frankly, I don't think we could ever entirely reproduce the experience of those Dublin days and nights. We can only trust *U2: The Early Days* proves to be a most acceptable substitute.

ACKNOWLEDGEMENTS

Much of the text obviously came from our memories, but many other people also helped in compiling it: Rob Partridge, Neil Storey, Annie Roseberry, Chas De Whalley, Charlie Eyre, Tom Nolan, Kieran and Cathy Owens, Gerry Leonard, Stan Erraught, Ross Fitzsimons, Andrew Whiteway, Dave Kavanagh, Mannix Flynn, Brummie and Conal Kearney. Obviously all opinions are solely the author's.

Also invaluable to research were Regine Moylett at Island's Press Office, and the staff at Principle Management: Barbara Galavan, Suzanne Doyle, Jackie Bennett and Eileen Long. Equally indispensable were the files of *Hot Press*, which stimulated many new leads and also helped sort out many chronological problems. Through their friendship and contributions over many years, Gavin Friday, Guggi, Dik and Debbie Schow also played a significant part.

Others who helped in the creation and administration of this project were Keren Killoran (for the idea), Laurie Katoilsil (sorry!), Robert Allen (introduction), Clodagh Corcoran (advice and support), Jean O'Hanlon (typing), Tony O'Shea (darkroom), Micheal O'Higgins (Legal Beagle), Paul Daly (special effects), and 'Percy' for coming into our lives and without whom ... etc.

Bill Graham would especially like to thank Niall Stokes and everyone at *Hot Press* for their comradeship for over a decade, and Roger Armstrong for his example, friendship and stimulus for even longer.

Three others merit a line to themselves. First, our agent and editor, Amy Garvey, both for her early enterprise and then for her patience, endurance and cups of rose-hip tea in seeing this project through. Second, Robin Robertson at Secker & Warburg. He was the first to see the potential of this book and rarely interfered, instead backing our rather special Irish demands. Third, Anne Louise Kelly at Principle Management. This project might still be grounded without her help.

But finally, U2 and Paul McGuinness. All gave their goodwill at crucial moments. We only single out Bono, Larry and Paul for their contributions because they were the pointsmen when we needed assistance: 'It's a long way from waking up with a tear on the tongue!'

Dublin, 26 February 1980. U2 are playing the National Stadium to an admiring throng of friends and fans. Bono proudly introduces 'Another Day', their second single for CBS Ireland, predicting, 'It won't be out on the CBS label for long. I can tell you that story.'

He isn't glibly boasting. Bono knows, you see. He knows that among the 1,200 at the Stadium is an aristocratically mannered Englishman, Bill Stewart, head of A & R at Island, and he's about to sign U2. It didn't matter much that Island would eventually pass on 'Another Day' and open U2's account with the Martin Hannett produced '11 O'Clock Tick Tock'. Bono's speaking the symbolic truth. U2 have cracked it. They've finally won a serious long-term recording contract, that Holy Grail that had eluded most of their Irish contemporaries.

Theirs has also been a most precocious success. Except for Adam Clayton, U2's members are still in their teens. Two years ago, Larry Mullen and the Edge were still students at Mount Temple, while Bono was finishing an extra school year to get the Irish-language qualification that would allow him to enter university. In these two intervening years, U2 have passed all their local tests. They've established the basics of a unique style, founded on Bono's theatrical presentation and the Edge's ringing guitar. They've also found an ambitious and equally astute manager in Paul McGuinness and a more sizeable, committed audience than any of their Dublin contemporaries – victories won against local apathy and even some enmity.

So U2 can celebrate on this Tuesday night. And not just because of Bill Stewart's presence, inviting them to Island. Young, unsigned Irish bands aren't meant to play the National Stadium. It's for securely popular acts, traditional music institutions like the Chieftains or the Bothy Band, or country artists like Emmylou Harris or Merle Haggard if they're passing through town. Yet here are U2, proclaiming their party, welcoming their 1,200 to the Stadium, showing they count in Dublin. Two months away from his twentieth birthday, Bono takes a step back from the microphone and then speaks, mingling his pride with late teenage adolescent awe: 'We're here in the Stadium. Big lights, big record-player, the whole beans.'

So, tonight, U2 can conduct their own city's symphony. Before 'Shadows and Tall Trees' – the tall trees, those slim amber street-lamps that lay their spectral lights and shadows on the night-life hopes of

Dublin youth – Bono will comment, 'Dim the lights, we feel embarrassed,' and then try out a tin whistle for a few callow, squirting phrases.

On, 'A Day Without Me', later to be their second Island single, he injects a couplet about his girlfriend and future wife, Alison Stewart: 'If Alison's dreaming, what's at stake?' His vocals aren't yet polished. On 'Stories For Boys' he's almost a Bowie soundalike, as if the laughing gnome had lodged in his throat. But mostly, there's a straining breathlessness, as if he's gulping at experiences that can be neither swallowed nor digested.

At the Stadium, U2 are still self-consciously and intentionally juvenile. But not juvenile delinquents. This is a band who have diverged from punk's bad boy and bad girl models. Bono prefers to play the Fool – incidentally the title of an early and unrecorded U2 song – a role he claims is borrowed from studying Shakespeare at school. Bono's Fool plays up to and with adolescent confusion, scurrying around the stage on 'Boy/Girl' like a hyperactive and over-impressionable manikin on his first date. For U2 are a strange paradox, they're actually confessing to and using uncoolness, vulnerability and insecurity as artistic devices when nearly all their contemporaries slap on a mask.

A paradox that had already confused many, it would continue to do so through so much of U2's career. They had reversed the terms. Other bands – and not only in Ireland – would cultivate images of poise and control and then be outmanoeuvred by the music business. Yet U2, and especially Bono, who never feared to play the gauche Fool, would retain control where it counted and rarely be outplayed.

Yet coupled with their feeling of triumph that night, their sense of achievement in convincing both Island's Bill Stewart and the other 1,200 in the Stadium, there was a deep sigh of relief. For U2's first two years involved an audacious gamble in their determination to design their career as they desired. The U2 paradox of being oddly normal had made them controversial creatures, a band who had both divided their own home scene in Dublin and generated no small degree of incomprehension in the British record companies who had first hoped and then hesitated to sign them.

Instinctively and incurably romantic and utopian, U2 had gone against the grain of those punk attitudes that, by 1980, were hardening into marginalization and antisocial cynicism. Or – that paradox again – as Bono confessed, introducing another unrecorded song and most consciously echoing John Lennon, 'The Dream Is Over.'

Yet if, like the hippie dream Lennon had lamented, the punk fantasy was now over, U2's own romance was only just beginning. They had bypassed their Dublin competitors. Through the eighties, they would gradually overhaul and then outpace all but a handful of their UK counterparts. It is highly arguable that their early isolated Irish experiences both hardened U2 and gave them the hunger for the task.

By their genes, by their early essential bloodings, ye shall know a band. U2 were born into a scene that was a blank slate, and they had the bravado and instinctive insight to scrawl their own signature on the board. They found their own fulfilment by recognizing that they weren't tied by rigid expectations of what rock should or shouldn't be. Beginning in a backwater, U2 would redefine Ireland's often incoherent aspirations.

Outside Ireland, U2 would initially be viewed as another post-punk provincial prodigy regularly associated with Simple Minds and Echo and the Bunnymen to the latter's oft-quoted dismay. And from the same vantage point, the pre-punk Dublin of '76 would have seemed little different from any lacklustre provincial British city where lethargic hippie survivors shuffled round a limited pub circuit, its musos the remnants of yet another scene that the London A & R men would have forgotten but for the fact that they had hardly bothered to notice it in the first place.

Yet, in many respects, Dublin had more in common with Continental European cities, closer in its lack of amenities and its patchwork rock tradition to Antwerp or Helsinki than Aberdeen or Cardiff. Like those Continental cities, the summit of pop ambition was victory at the annual Eurovision Song Contest. The light-entertainment values that had been routed in Britain since the mid-sixties, still held sway over rock. Typically until a network of pirate radio stations emerged in '77, there wasn't even a national pop radio channel.

Free lunch-time concerts in Trinity College Dublin during rag week, May 1979. Despite the rain the crowd stay to listen. The band rarely missed an opportunity to promote themselves, so just in case anyone was in doubt who was playing, the joker on stage is wearing a sandwich board of U2's poster

This impoverishment may have given U2 their ambition, the sense that they had more to prove. It may be no coincidence that both Bob Geldof and U2 were over-achievers. Certainly U2's ambition could make them overcompensate and overshoot their mark. Equally their mistakes, or at least those aspects that usually most troubled their critics, generally involved exaggeration and overemotional statement. This wasn't necessarily due to some abstract racial Celtic characteristic, but resulted as much from the forces that shaped Irish popular culture.

Now, in 1989, U2 sit astride the global charts far above their immediate British rivals from the early eighties. Detractors can point to calculated marketing, and certainly nobody could claim that U2 lack awareness of the finer arts of professional persuasion. But again such talk can obscure the forces that shaped them. Escaping from a vacuum, the 'nowhere' on the rock map that was Ireland, U2 soon learned to seize their own state of independence.

Indeed, it is arguable that their first task in getting signed was U2's most difficult challenge. Very early on, U2 were a hardened band, perhaps harder than even they knew when they signed with Island. Very early on, they found dedication, an accompanying mental toughness, and the ability to appreciate and select the essentials of any situation. Plus a set of especially Irish cultural codes that would regularly puzzle those critics who would equally regularly underestimate the band since U2 have always approached rock issues from their own oblique Irish angle.

Now, ten years later, biographers should be careful and beware of the memories of their informants. Especially when the small change of the famous is involved, few can resist the temptation to inflate their roles as bit part players and claim key interventions in the plot. And even if the star attractions try to testify honestly, memory can play them false and turn to myth as symbolic truths replace the facts.

Even simple matters of chronology can get muddled. I should recall where and when I first saw U2 playing and then spin a tale of instant conversion as if I'd been blinded by the spirit of the resurrected Elvis Presley on the rocky road to Damascus.

After all, I introduced them to their manager and spent a month's campaign of persuasion, often over bottles of cheap red Burgundy in a Dublin night-club called Pierre's, laying siege to an initially sceptical Paul McGuinness.

But actually I can't remember that first date. I can recall how, when and why I first met them – another matter entirely – but my first three or four dates with U2 are now a blur, a jumble of impressions from all those shows.

Later Bono would talk of U2 using 'the primary colours' of rock in their classic four-man line-up, and the basic elements were there from the start. Whereas in the spring of '78 every other young Dublin guitarist was still trying to emulate the pneumatic-drill rhythm style of punk, the Edge even then preferred bursts of quicksilver chiming melody. And Bono already had an insatiable compulsion to communicate. Totally unable to freeze into any studied pose, he could be jabberingly eager, always likely to overrun a verse or chorus and destroy the others' cues and timing with some spontaneous vocal or stage stunt. Through Bono, U2 rejected rock's manneredness. Never afraid to look flustered or foolish – in many ways, the worst crime in the book of rules – Bono was reversing rock's ideas of sophistication.

Later he would conceive of himself as 'an offering to the audience' and he already had the ability to rivet their attention. Of course, with that magnetism there were many mistakes. But Bono learned to use them; he rarely repeated the same error.

Very soon, I started to bore everyone, my colleagues at *Hot Press* and other Dublin musicians, with my praise for the band. In time, people in Dublin would tell me I discovered U2. Untrue, since there are many more with a right to that claim: Steve Averill, Jackie Hayden, Dave McCullough, Chris Westwood, Rob Partridge, Annie Roseberry and Bill Stewart, to name only the most prominent. Or Chas De Whalley, Charlie Eyre and Tom Nolan, and the A & R scouts who tried and failed to sign U2 to respectively CBS, A & M, and EMI. The real truth is one every successful band knows – U2 were always rather skilled at discovering people to discover them!

They needed that persistence and persuasiveness in a scene with limited opportunities. Early U2 can't be understood without a detailed examination of their Irish background. For even the punk rebellion would have its own peculiarly ambiguous meanings specific to Ireland alone.

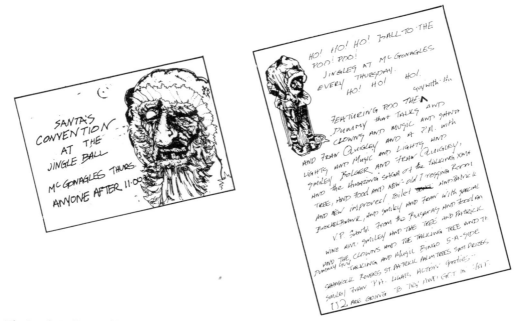

Above right: The Jingle Balls, a publicity stunt that caught attention. Christmas celebrations at Easter. A Thursday late-night residency in McGonagle's. The stage was adorned with Christmas decorations and for the first gig, slides were projected at the side of the stage of the Evans family. There were also night scenes, Dublin characters and trees, all taken by James Mahon

Dublin in 1989 is a very different scene from that into which U2 were initiated. Today if you walk through the Temple Bar area, just south of the Liffey, you'll hear in every alleyway, the din of hopeful bands, perfecting their sound in the neighbourhood's rehearsal rooms. Enter the Pink Elephant Club or the Baggot Inn and you'll regularly meet London A & R men, scouting for Dublin talent.

But, when U2 began, facilities like professional rehearsal rooms were non-existent and sympathetic London A & R men were equally notable by their absence. Now Dublin blooms with activity, then it was a desert through which U2 had to crawl on their way to the oasis of a contract.

So, when punk struck, its Irish supporters would have a rather different agenda from their UK counterparts. The British vanguard audience had been sated by rock. Knowing and self-conscious consumers, they were fleeing from rock, disillusioned because of their misplaced faith in the hippie generation whose promise of a radical community had degenerated into stadium rock with its increasingly blatant hierarchy.

But the Irish, still lacking the media and concert amenities the British took for granted, were starved of rock. Still innocent outsiders, they wanted to enter rock and use

it to attack and extinguish the peculiar dinosaurs of their own culture's creation. Chief among these was the showband, those indigenous Irish freaks and throwbacks of pop evolution, a phenomenon that absolutely dominated and distorted the Irish music business.

Essentially electrified mutations of the post-war dance bands slimmed down to about eight members, the showbands concentrated on cover versions. Beneficiaries of cultural protectionism in a land without any national or local pop stations, the showbands were the main vehicle by which UK and American pop was disseminated in Ireland – often with hilarious and unintentionally camp ineptitude. Not surprisingly, they took good care to respect the codes of conservative rural Irish Catholic morality, disguising and diluting rock's more outrageous and abandoned values.

They were also extremely protective of their monopoly. Showband managers would campaign against the hotel discos that emerged in rural Ireland throughout the seventies – ostensibly protesting because, unlike the unlicensed dancehalls, the discos served alcohol, but actually because their patrons could now hear foreign hit records without the aid of those travelling jukeboxes the showbands. And when RTE, the national television station, decided to transmit *Top of the Pops*, bands and managers even picketed the studios in a lather of outrage.

Obviously rock in all its varieties languished in Ireland. Like fearful East European cultural commissars, the showbands stifled creativity. Especially outside Dublin, there was hardly any place to play, and the showbands' economic stranglehold forced most innovative Irish musicians to emigrate to London or elsewhere. Furthermore, since the live performance of covers meant that the record wasn't the unit of Irish musical currency, showband profits were rarely reinvested in developing Irish music, so the installation of quality recording studios was delayed.

Other cultural factors also came into play. Rock was seen almost as an un-Irish activity of dubious colonial morality, an alien force that might undermine both an insecure national identity and Catholic ways. Thus rock was orphaned and disowned, reinforcing the hopeless lack of confidence and stagnation within Ireland's isolated community of long-hair musicians.

Horslips were the first band to try and break out of this state of bondage. Unlike their UK folk-rock counterparts, Horslips didn't deal in even-tempered elegies. Instead they married Irish traditional music to glam and pomp rock. This incongruous brew would make them a curious footnote outside Ireland, but in their homeland Horslips had a major commercial and cultural impact. They were the first Irish band to dent the showband monopoly in the ballrooms, giving a generation of rural Irish teenagers their first experience of live rock. But it fell to Bob Geldof and the Boomtown Rats to ignite Ireland and set new, ambitious standards for international success.

Ireland needed somebody like Geldof, with his over-compensation of ego, daring, bluster and impatience. The early unsigned Rats of '75 and '76, long before anyone in Ireland had heard of the Sex Pistols, swiftly divided the Dublin scene. They couldn't play their instruments, the local musicians fretted as if rock had always required a driver's licence to perform perfect, tiresome ten-minute solos. And Geldof's defiant boast that he wanted to be rich, famous and laid was an entirely intentional blast against

Bono came to the photo sessions with lots of ideas. In this shot, Bono wanted Patrick Brocklebank to catch him in full flight with the Edge and Adam sitting composed. It didn't happen but they had great fun in the attempt

hippie introspection and its sleepy laidback 'good vibes' and fear of success.

As elsewhere, however, a new, younger audience were discovering afresh that music could pay raucous witness to urban frustration and unsavoury violence. And with Thin Lizzy also regularly featuring in the British charts, there was a second model to inspire the new breed of Irish band that was emerging in the wake of punk. With the exception of the classy Radiators, however, they were essentially erratic power-pop bands – a good night's entertainment, but conceptually naive, immature and unoriginal. If new energies had been unleashed, they had yet to find a focus. That U2 would provide.

They weren't always called U2. The band who had started in Mount Temple when Larry Mullen had pinned his appeal for fellow musicians on the school notice-board had previously traded as Feedback and the Hype. It was Steve Averill, their first adviser and ally, who christened them U2.

Adam Clayton had sought him out through Steve's brother, Mark, a fellow Mount Temple student. An apathetic pupil even within Mount Temple's liberal regime, Adam devoted all his energies to directing the band's affairs, even composing congratulatory fan messages to the Hype for the classified columns of *New Musical Express.*

Steve Averill was a perfect adviser. Lead singer with the Radiators under his punk *nom de guerre,* Steve Rapid (he would later quit the band due to the twin demands of his marriage and his job as a designer in a Dublin advertising agency), he typified the aware, altruistic activists punk threw up everywhere. Initiating Dublin fanzines *Raw Power* and *Black and White* and always ready to advise any new band about image, direction or useful contacts, Steve was always nudging events along.

In early '78 he first saw the inexperienced teenage band, wearing mohair jumpers, playing Stranglers and Sex Pistols covers as a support in a Dublin bar. They were completely unformed. Steve thought Larry their strongest player, the best young drummer he'd seen in Dublin. The Edge was promising, but Bono was hurtling around the stage, not yet in control, while the Edge's elder brother, Dik, on second guitar, seemed superfluous.

Like so many others later, Steve first warmed to the band's level-headed attitude. Though all of them with the exception of Adam were still at school, they weren't hesitant students. They neither wound him up nor fawned. Instead they carefully weighed his advice and then firmly and rationally made their own decisions. Adam regularly walked the two miles along the shore from his Malahide home, if only to con a social cup of coffee and glean the latest gossip from Steve in Portmarnock. It all added to the pose, to the grand teenage dream that the Hype were somehow significant.

But that dire, dreadfully unpunky name, the Hype, had to go – especially since, in March '78, the band were planning their first step up the local ladder. They entered a Limerick talent contest, co-sponsored by Harp Lager and CBS, for which the first prize would be £500 – useful money to any band in '78 – and a demo session funded by CBS.

Adam favoured XTC as a model, since the Swindon band's name was both simple and versatile. Steve suggested U2, but though an early favourite it was by no means a foregone conclusion. Because they were still at school, the Blazers, the joke name on Steve's list, might be equally apt. But it was U2 who played and won at Limerick, their closest competition an older Dublin R & B band, the East Coast Angels. That St Patrick's Day victory would have two consequences: impressing their first record company supporter, Jackie Hayden of CBS, and also alerting me to their existence.

I didn't see their next date at the Howth Community Centre. Bottom of the bill, the five-man Hype with Dik played their final set before Dik bowed out. Now studying engineering at Trinity College, the elder Evans had happily let kid brother Dave take over all the guitar duties in the new model U2 that finished the show.

They were still raw. Sharper punk fans would chide them for the venial sin against fashion of covering Thin Lizzy's 'Dancing in the Moonlight' but that was a definite advance on the early Feedback and Hype covers of Peter Frampton's 'Show Me The Way' and the Moody Blues' 'Nights In White Satin'. As U2 matured, so would their covers with Wire's 'Mannequin' entering the set while the Ramones' 'Glad To See You Go'

often featured as an encore.

Equally significant was the rest of the bill. Adam played bass for Steve's own synth band while Larry joined him in the rhythm section of the other band, U2's co-conspirators, the Virgin Prunes. Later when tales that U2 were born-again Christians began to circulate, the Dublin scene would be mystified by their continuing association with the Dada transvestite provocateurs, the Virgin Prunes. How, people wondered, could apparent Cliff Richard clones fraternize with the most outrageous and outwardly decadent band in town?

That link was Lypton Village. Boys would be boys and bond together in this secretive, ceremonial if informal grouping that included members of both bands. Led by Bono and the Prunes' two singers, Guggi (Derek Rowan) and Gavin Friday (Fionan Hanvey), Lypton Village was a refuge, a defence against all the conventional roles demanded from young Dublin males, which allowed them to dream and to refuse to grow up as Irish society expected. Lypton Village had its own arcane games, special Village Olympics on the North Dublin seashore, contests like 'walking the rice paper', a Monty Pythonesque silly walk that parodied Kung Fu. Or the two Virgin Prunes singers, Gavin Friday and Guggi would go 'collecting heads', searching for idiosyncratic and slightly crazed characters on the streets of Dublin.

It also christened people and initiated them into their alternative identities. Thus the Edge came from a hardware store Bono passed on his bus trips into town. Also Bono, of course, from an O'Connell Street hearing-aid shop. The singer was most fortunate: his previous Lypton Village name had been Steinhegvanhuysenolegbangbangbangbang. Steinhegvanhuysenolegbangbangbangbang and the Blazers? Hardly a name to set the world alight!

Musically Bono and the Virgin Prunes' leader, Gavin Friday (Fionan Hanvey), were close. Bono's home contained no record player, only an unwieldy reel-to-reel tape machine. He had first been impressed by his elder brother Norman's tapes of the Cream, the Who, and Jimi Hendrix. Like Gavin, he'd then become a fan of David Bowie. Now Gavin, together with his friend Tommy McCann (the Bottle of Milk in Lyptonese),

Guggi and Gavin Friday lead singers of the Virgin Prunes at McGonagle's 26 May 1979
insert: Bono and Gavin share the microphone in a duet with Guggi backing on the right. Project Arts Centre, 18 September 1978

were the Village's record collectors. First on the block with the latest independent obscurities, Gavin's house became the setting for Bono's musical education.

In time, the pair would even use the same song titles. Gavin wrote a song called 'Boy/Girl' and Bono reciprocated a fortnight later with a similarly named song. Both wrote songs called 'Another Time, Another Place' and 'Johnny Swallow', and the Prunes' debut piece at Howth Community Centre was 'Exit', a title Bono would use years later on 'The Joshua Tree'.

Another example of Village creative incest was '11 O'Clock Tick Tock', U2's first Island single. Bono arrived home late one night after missing a meeting with Gavin to find a note with '11 O'Clock Tick Tock' pinned to the front door. Even the song's chorus, 'I hear the children crying', would be used by the Prunes as a title on their debut 'If I Die I Die' album on Rough Trade.

The two bands definitely saw each other as complementary. Gavin Friday would press Hugo McGuinness to do his first photo session with U2, while Bono would help recruit the Prunes' first manager, Kieran Owens. Owens, who later managed the Dublin bands Cactus World News and the Fountainhead, recalls an early meeting with the pair in a Dublin restaurant where Bono insisted that U2 would be the mainstream band while the Prunes would aim for the outsiders and misfits U2 could never hope to reach, something like the relationship that existed between David Bowie and Iggy Pop.

The timing of that conversation was also important. Early '78 was the post-punk moment, that time of crisis, opportunity and musical promiscuity after Johnny Rotten had quit the Sex Pistols. The punk vanguard had moved on, experimenting with Ska, rockabilly, mod and dub, or turning to new art bands like Kraftwerk, the Pop Group, Suicide and Père Ubu. U2 would start their ascent just as the hectic turnover of post-punk styles would create a new tribalism of warring fashion and music factions. Discernment and selectivity, the stealth and instinct to scramble through the post-punk maze would now become the guiding values.

U2 were never punks. Though Bono might be fascinated by Johnny Rotten and U2 would gain through the movement's

opportunities, the safety-pin uniform would have been utterly false for students from one of Dublin's most progressive schools.

Even if the foursome were uneasy about Ireland, there were no obvious targets for rebellion. If Bob Geldof had wanted revenge for his oppressive Catholic education, U2's school was tolerant and multi-denominational. Why, the fledgling band had even been encouraged by some of their Mount Temple teachers!

Overt political rebellion didn't make much sense either. It presupposed that every teenage band had as much time and opportunity to swot up on socialism and anarchisms to master their music. Unlike Britain, Ireland actually experienced a short if deceptive period of economic expansion from '77 to '79, so the Clash's tower-block imagery didn't gel. Bono and Larry might live near to Ireland's lone high-rise housing project, Ballymun, which much later would be 'The Seven Towers' of 'Running to Stand Still', but none of the band had known poverty. And the Northern Ireland troubles were far removed from the experience of Southern teenagers – if anything, a television turn-off.

If British punk screamed 'No future', Irish youth had more reason to shout 'No past', scorning what the Radiators called the 'made to measure' history of Catholicism and atavistic nationalism still taught at that time in most Irish classrooms. Besides, rebellion for its own sake could seem like a traditional Irish trap. Yet again Irish needs were compiling a different agenda from Britain.

Irish folk musicians like Christy Moore and Moving Hearts would be the first to be explicitly political when they supported the H-Block hunger strikers. But Irish rock, both before and after punk, was agnostic between the competing creeds of Unionism and Catholic nationalism. The Northern Irish punk bands like Stiff Little Fingers and the groups gathered around the Undertones on the Good Vibrations label, were fighting for a genuinely non-sectarian social space, searching for a sanctuary where Northern punks could abandon their Catholic and Protestant identities and pogo together as fellow fans.

Adrift and detached from the nation's political culture, Irish rock could only be vaguely anti-authoritarian. To paraphrase Yeats, rock alone was certain good. In the eighties, partly through U2's own unprecedented success, these relationships would become less innocent and grow ever more complex, but in the late seventies the very act of joining a band set one apart in Ireland.

Yet U2 were themselves untypical. Not just in their family background, with two Protestants – Adam Clayton and the Edge, the second son of the Welsh Evans family. Christened Paul Hewson, Bono was the child of a mixed marriage. Only Larry Mullen came from a conventional Catholic family. Furthermore, Mount Temple itself was an oasis, a unique school that protected them from the guilt and scar-tissue of a Catholic education. And since Mount Temple was also a co-educational school, again unique in Ireland in the late seventies, U2 were also spared those stereotypical Irish problems with girls. This portrait of these Irish artists as young men could never follow James Joyce's model of sexual and spiritual repression.

Thus U2 would never have the obvious Irish starting points. They would be compelled to rely absolutely on their own individual romantic and spiritual adolescent confusions for their themes. After all, punk had defined its own rules and limits by making love songs and confessions of vulnerability taboo. U2 would try to separate teen traumas and aspirations from brittle punk nihilism.

But in early '78, U2 were just another aerosol-sprayed name on Dublin's hoardings. They had neither found their audience nor caused any ripples of notoriety. To the city's competing cliques U2, the Virgin Prunes and Lypton Village were unknown outsiders.

The circle who supported the Radiators prided themselves on being the most hip. Mostly from the Navan Road district in north-west Dublin, they claimed the pedigree of having bought the touchstone American punk albums by the Stoodges, New York Dolls and MC5 as far back as '75. They shunned the Boomtown Rats – Bob Geldof's courtship of publicity was suspect. Likewise his magpie opportunism and pilfering of punk emblems.

The violence however, was purely verbal. Dublin's first punk purists played up to their image, but never confused it with reality. Besides, the Radiators had already learnt their tragic lesson. In summer '77, the band had organized and headlined a four-band show at Dublin's second university, University College Dublin, during which there was a fatal stabbing at the back of the hall, the victim dying of a punctured lung in the ambulance on the way to hospital. The Undertones, who had made their first trip to Dublin for this event, actually fell under suspicion – to the Gardai, punk plus Derry was a lethal equation – and were quizzed by the RUC on their return home. Yet when the police traced the killer, he was found to be a seventeen-year-old malcontent nobody knew.

Immediately punk was barred from the city's venues. Moran's, the forging ground for both the Rats and the Radiators, had temporarily closed down for financial reasons and soon irretrievably lost its reputation. The other pub venue, the Baggot Inn, backed off, preferring older bands, those Eagles and Steely Dan fans who'd taken from the Cars to update their image and play a kinder, gentler and entirely spurious New Wave.

The next watershed came in late '77. When the Clash arrived in Dublin as the first British punk band to play Ireland, the première happened in the venerable liberal setting of Trinity College's eighteenth-century Exam Hall. The Dublin scene harboured many absurdities, but few were more incongruous than the Clash evading the pogoers' spittle beneath the hall's organ loft and the paintings of the University's founder, Queen Elizabeth I, on the oak-panelled walls.

Yet despite the gobbers, this was a well-heeled student not a boot boy audience. In essence, the working-class housing estates remained loyal to hard rock – to Thin Lizzy, Rory Gallagher, Status Quo and Judas Priest. Only middle-class brats could afford to buy records and equipment and gain parental consent, however reluctant, to form a band. And in the various groups – skinny-tie New Wave, not punk – would be the son of an Abbey Theatre director, relatives of an RTE Orchestra conductor and even the children of a past-President of the Irish Rugby Football Union.

Dublin definitely wasn't a centre of dole-queue rock. Neither was there much originality among the second-hand Dublin beat groups then venturing out. Certainly I found none to champion before I met U2 for the first time in early April '78, about three weeks after the band's St Patrick's Day victory in the Limerick talent contest. Somehow Adam had got hold of my home phone number and was personally plaguing my mother, but it was the Limerick news that decided me to take a 31 bus and meet them on a Saturday afternoon in the Green Dolphin, a bar near Mount Temple.

I liked them right away. There was no empty bluster. They didn't pretend to any grand musical plan. As Steve Averill had found, they asked simple practical questions. In time what would most impress Paul McGuinness about his new charges was what he termed their 'lack of waste'. Of course, that's how they presented themselves to us. If U2 ever had any disputes between themselves, the four never revealed those rifts, always putting on an impressive show of solidarity for outsiders. They would later claim their career was never so controlled and that they were much more hot-headed. Perhaps that was their own daily experience but for an observer like myself, even then U2 appeared unfailingly to concentrate their attention on the next rung of the ladder.

Paul McGuinness would become the other element in the equation. He was my only Trinity colleague in the Dublin scene, and we naturally gravitated to each other. After midnight in Pierre's, he would 'elaborate' – Paul's favourite word then – his schemes for orchestrating his deal of deals. His managerial philosophy was then more traditional. Paul didn't exactly scorn punk but he certainly suspected it. For Paul, it couldn't generate careers. Yet its energy had affected him. What, Paul began to wonder, would it be like managing a young band from scratch?

I can't recall when or where I first saw U2 play. I do know it wasn't infatuation at first sight, more a gradual appreciation of their potential. Bono certainly had an irrepressible candour and energy, but it was the Edge's playing that first drew me.

I'd had my fill of electric skiffle guitarists scratching out rhythmic clichés. They probably believed they were emulating the Pistols' Steve Jones, Paul Weller or Joe Strummer, but in truth all you heard were transparent, inept variations on Keith Richards's 'Sticky Fingers' riff. But with his snatches of snaky melodic phrases, the Edge already had the first elements of a distinctive style. While all the other bands sprinted through their sets at maximum velocity, U2 dared to pause for an emotive breather in the slow atmospherics of 'Shadows and Tall Trees'.

They also suited my theories. I might appreciate the Ramones and the Clash, but I preferred the Jam just because they were young while the older pair of bands were inevitably self-conscious. Punk, I thought, had become too knowing and self-referential. I believed teenage bands could evolve existentially, out of a natural inner compulsion, whereas their elder brothers and sisters had already found their basic adult identity, creating from fashion and their record collections and not from the experiences younger bands shared with their audiences.

The Jam were also my ideal working model because I loved Paul Weller's dictum, stuck to his guitar, 'Standards Rule', for its impartial disdain towards both hippie and punk self-indulgence. And if the Jam could latch on to mod, why couldn't their successors go forward to the eclectic pre-psychedelic guitar pop of '66? The Jam's 'Away From the Numbers' and Cream's 'I Feel Free' became the prisms through which I viewed the early U2 sound.

So went my crude and close to contradictory theories in early '78. What I do know is that I couldn't abide any more heroic Irish failures. Given the backwardness of Irish popular culture, success was an ally not an enemy.

Besides, the punk watershed disguised another crucial qualitative changes in the Dublin scene. From '77, a small cabal of graduates essentially from both Dublin universities would emerge as the new leadership. Niall and Dermot Stokes would create *Hot Press*. Ossie Kilkenny would become Dublin's leading music business accountant. James Morris and Meiert Avis would be among Windmill Lane Studios' founders. Dave Fanning would become Ireland's leading rock disc-jockey. Dave Kavanagh would move from being U2's first Irish agent to become Clannad's manager, while Billy Magra would fill various roles as promoter and manager before settling into television and video production. They shared no common allegiance to the new music. But what united all of them was a determination to reshape the Irish music business, to end both the showbands' outmoded rule and Ireland's isolation. All would enter the U2 story to a greater or lesser degree by providing elements of the infrastructure that allowed the band to remain in Ireland. All would see U2's success as the justification of their endeavours.

All would have shared rather than sneered at Paul McGuinness's ambitions. My personal myth has it that I had a lengthy campaign to recruit a reluctant McGuinness to manage U2. Again memory plays me false, for U2 won the Limerick talent competition on March 17, met me in early April, and on May 25, Paul saw the band at the Project Arts Centre and agreed to work with them.

But the alliance with Paul McGuinness immediately led to suspicions in a scene still imbued with notions of punk amateurism. U2 were thought pampered, falsely and flagrantly flash and middle-class, while Paul's impatience with cant could initially border on tactlessness. In July, U2 were due to play McGonagle's bottom of the bill beneath Steve Averill's band, the Modern

Heirs and Revolver. Paul didn't want U2 to play before the crowd arrived so he fought to switch them above their mentor's band. A compromise was reached. U2 did play first but their start was delayed. As the headliners, Revolver retained the best time-slot but the Modern Heirs played last, albeit late into the morning when the audience were either addled, apathetic or absent. Steve grumbled to the *Hot Press* but bore no lasting grudge. Others, usually with less reason, would be less tolerant of U2 and their manager, whom Lypton Village had already christened the Goose.

Guggi with Paul 'The Goose' McGuinness

James Mahon was the first of our three photographers to snap U2. Between the ages of four and eleven he had attended Glasnevin Primary School with Bono and the two became good friends. James recalls watching the television coverage of the American space missions at the Hewson home. But he didn't accompany Bono to Mount Temple. Living two miles away, the pair drifted apart, and it was only because his sister Isobel knew Adam's sister, Cindy, that he renewed contact. Soon afterwards he bluffed his way into McGonagle's, pretending to be a professional photographer where U2 were again supporting Revolver.

Managed by Terry O'Neill, McGonagle's had replaced Moran's as Dublin's leading club. It was ill-lit and scruffy, served paint-stripper wine, and its stage featured incongruous and intrusive plastic palm trees, a kitsch relic from its previous incarnation as a dingy disco. While other venues were still wary of the new scene, Terry O'Neill welcomed and relished the colour and social anarchy.

It was also the site of U2's first breakthrough, supporting Advertising. A second-line EMI power-pop band, Advertising were ideal rivals for U2 to test their progress against. Despite the Rats' and Lizzy's commercial success, Dublin bands still felt inferior to London visitors. U2 didn't. They didn't blow Advertising away, but they easily and confidently matched them. Certainly I recall it as the night when I first believed U2 might just be specially gifted.

The next test was when U2 supported the Stranglers before their biggest audience yet at the Top Hat ballroom on September 9. With no dressing room of their own, they changed behind the stage. Without a sound check, the Edge's guitar amp spluttered with static and when he broke a string, Bono had an uphill battle against the Stranglers' fans who gobbed him and threw lighted cigarettes on the stage. But he didn't shrivel. The band only got £50 and the bonus of some bottles of wine that they liberated from the Stranglers' dressing room, but it had been a necessary blooding before a hostile audience. Facing them down, they had definitely won some new friends.

One of them was Patrick Brocklebank, whose first encounter with U2 this was. A photographer with *In Dublin* magazine, he'd gone to see the Stranglers but was sufficiently impressed by U2 to take over thirty shots of them. Then coincidence intervened. The following week, his brother Aidan was driving back from Cork and picked up Adam, hitch-hiking with his girlfriend Donna. Aidan was in the second-hand car business. 'Oh' said Adam, 'perhaps you could find us a van. I'll give you a phone call.' Of course the call was answered by Patrick, who told Adam of his photos and was immediately invited down to U2's next date at the Project Arts Centre on September 18.

U2's defiant attitude when supporting the Stranglers' had proved their mettle. No longer some abstract schoolyard dream, they were now beginning to realize their strengths, themes and identity. And just in time, since the Dublin scene was about to enter its next stormy phase.

Only now, after the summer of '78, was punk percolating through the city's housing estates, long after Johnny Rotten had spat himself out of the Sex Pistols and Sid Vicious had become the band's icon. Long after its early moment of controversy, punk had become populist and its original champions had moved on. When the Clash returned to Dublin to play the Top Hat in October, it would be as symbolic as their Trinity debut.

But not because of the Clash. Instead the Virgin Prunes, U2's most art-terrorist allies, in their first major Dublin performance, dramatically drew the line. Cross-dressed in black stockings, Guggi and Gavin Friday mimed sex, and faced a stage invasion when Gavin's clothes ripped (unintentionally, he claims) to expose his genitals which inflamed the audience. After twenty minutes of white noise provocation including the Prunes' audience – baiting speciality 'Art Fuck', the stage was invaded and the harassed promoter pulled the plugs. A letter writer to *Hot Press* would chide the outraged punks who thought the Prunes queers and therefore beyond salvation: 'Punks are supposed *to* shock, not *be* shocked by their contemporaries.'

The Prunes were only reflecting the fracture of the punk consensus, now blindingly obvious in Britain. Johnny Rotten's PIL would be symbolically ranged against those in thrall to Sid Vicious' heedless tearaway image. Punk had managed to unify both aesthetic middle-class and political working-class styles of revolt but now those two streams were diverging. The Prunes definitely preferred PIL. Gavin Friday, whose favourite record was then an album of ridiculous Sex Pistols covers by Spanish session musicians, relished parody as provocation. The Prunes were stamping on standard Irish models of masculinity. They hated punk degenerating into heavy metal hooliganism.

So did U2. The insurrection seemed to have petrified into a set of stock attitudes. The 'Boy' of their debut album would be a 'Boy', never a lad. But if the Prunes hurt, U2

Bill Graham interviews U2 and the Virgin Prunes about Lypton Village in the Willows, a house in Glasnevin rented by the Rowan brothers and Lypton Village's HQ, March 1979

healed. They eschewed confrontation preferring more subtle, inclusive means of communication.

The Prunes also brought Hugo McGuinness into play. At art school and as a regular supplier of photos to the London music magazines, Hugo had seen the Pistols in Copenhagen in late '76. Since then no Dublin band had impressed him till he saw the Prunes at the Top Hat and started working with them. Gavin suggested he also help U2, but Hugo's first sighting of them was a débâcle. Supporting Phil Lynott's Greedy Bastards, a conglomeration of Thin Lizzy and the Pistols' Jones and Cook, U2 were all muffled, incoherent sound in a set plagued by technical problems. Hugo would only recognize their potential in the following spring as U2 finally went into overdrive.

The Greedy Bastards setback did not make for Christmas cheer, but generally U2 had cause for New Year celebrations. They had survived their early initiation tests, found a manager and established a Dublin presence, and their progress was confirmed when they packed McGonagle's on January 3, '79.

There was one obstacle to increasing their Dublin following: the licensing laws that forbade under eighteens attending clubs like McGonagle's. Through the spring and summer of '79, U2 found their solution on Saturday afternoons at the Dandelion, a disused indoor car park next to the Gaiety Green flea market beside St Stephen's Green.

The organizer, John Fisher, followed a strict and spartan policy. Any band could play provided they accepted the low entrance price of fifty pence or one pound. All that was needed was a sound desk, a basic lighting-rig and amplification on a low, rickety wooden stage, the bands, and whoever they could attract to the dilapidated premises. The market had also become the weekend magnet for all the city's new tribes. Punks, rockabillies, skinheads and mods would gather in the Green or the neighbouring streets and face each other down, though there was rarely any rumpus.

Previously dismissive, Hugo McGuinness was converted at the Dandelion. Ten minutes into U2's set, Adam's and the Edge's sound failed. As helpers scurried around with their screwdrivers, most bands would have temporarily sidelined themselves. Not one with Bono in it. He called a kid up from the crowd and hummed him the bass line. He explained a crude version of the Edge's part to another. Then as Larry whacked away and the understudies mouthed the instrumental lines, Bono improvised the lyrics before the electricity returned. It was hardly Pink Floyd at Pompeii, but Bono's stroke of bravado was enough to win Hugo over.

Bono's spontaneity was increasingly founded on craft. With Gavin Friday, he had been learning elementary theatrical techniques from Mannix Flynn and Conal Kearney. Mannix, actor and writer, found his vocation in theatre when serving time in prison. A visiting theatre group inspired him so much that when he was released he sought them out and within a year was acting in a play he had written himself. Conal Kearney was a graduate of the Abbey School of Acting and was one of the first Irish artists to study mime with the great Marcel Marceau. The sessions were short-lived and casual but Bono and Gavin gleaned the basics – like how to use body language, how to eye and control an audience and time their effects. If nothing else, the sessions confirmed the pair's thoroughness and determination.

They also helped Bono develop his early routines. During 'Boy/Girl' he would gesture to someone from the audience to hand him an unlit cigarette and then rush round the stage, casting himself as the bewildered, insecure teen with his first illicit smoke, a cameo supposed to dramatize all the secret cravings before the boy met manhood.

Then there was Elsie, a Lypton Village discovery. They'd found her during their Beautiful People spell (Village shorthand for a phase when they were fascinated by Dublin's more misfit characters). In her late thirties, Elsie knew nothing about rock but she'd attached herself to U2. So at the end of each set, Elsie had her five minutes of fame, awkwardly waltzing with the gallant Bono.

U2 played the Dandelion hardly half-a-

above left: The Dandelion: despite the derelict surroundings U2 attracted a large audience and, though they played the venue only five or six times, it was these gigs that gave them their following, establishing them as Dublin's most promising and popular band. *above:* Elsie pulls Adam's leg and wins her five minutes of fame

Guggi attempts to readjust his stockings with a helping hand from Adam

dozen times but these shows definitely built their Dublin audience. They also confirmed their manager's faith in the band. Initially unsure of U2, Paul McGuinness now marked one particularly enthralling show by giving Bono a bottle of champagne to spray all over the audience at the encore, the first instance of a ritual continued to this day on special occasions. But he could still be confused and impatient with Lypton Village antics. After one Dandelion show, Gavin Friday took over the stage for a long, keening, shapeless performance. This was amateurish indulgence, fumed McGuinness, who was grievously tempted to pull Gavin off the stage.

Certainly these weren't standard rock ceremonies. U2 refused to take their style from any of the various tribes that gathered round the Dandelion. Musically, too, they strove to censor received ideas from their songs. The Edge would claim he could easily write Jam or Cars songs; the real problem, he'd calmly continue, was excising such obvious influence from U2's music.

From anyone else, it would have been windy bluff, but U2 were becoming a force, and the scene had to reckon with them. Yet the band were distrusted. With the exception of Adam, they rarely socialized in the bars like the Bailey, Bruxelles and the Toby Jug where other bands drank to their dreams. They seemed too sensible and much too ambitious. Tales began to circulate, confided in tones that were half-appalled, half-bemused – U2 were born-again Christians!

I had dismissed or knew nothing of those rumours when I did my first lengthy *Hot Press* interview at the Prunes' Willows House in February '79, a session divided into three, intended to spotlight Lypton Village and the Prunes as well as U2. For the first twenty minutes, Bono gaily elaborated on Village rituals. Then without any prompting, he suddenly volunteered to my tape recorder: 'One other thing you should know about the Village – we're all Christians.'

I never used those unforced revelations. Afterwards, walking to the bus stop with Bono and Gavin, I had struggled to state the reasons for my protective discretion and found them to be all paradoxes. I, a typically Irish ex-Catholic agnostic, feared for their reputation. Born-again Christianity could hinder their career – a view which, the more I pondered it, was riven with illogicalities.

After all, 'Falling down gets you accepted' was among the period's favourite one-liners. This was a time when heroin still held a romantically tempting allure for those who supposed themselves street existentialists. Self-destructive behaviour could still win credibility and headlines. Even repentance by the reformed prodigal could gain further approving column inches. But the reverse wasn't true. Contrariwise, U2 might be pilloried for their religious beliefs and win no extra credit if and when they repudiated them.

Besides, it might be – convenient words – 'only a phase'. Lypton Village wouldn't have been the first late adolescent clique to reinforce their collective identity by bonding around an unpopular cause or cult. With others, it had been the Provisionals or conspiratorial far-left groups. Or Eastern sects like the supermarket mysticism of the Guru Maharishi's Divine Light cult which, earlier in the seventies, had borne off many Irish musicians. No sense then in exposing people with so much time to learn and mature.

In time, outsiders would look at U2, combine the categories of 'Ireland' and 'Religion', and mistakenly make a Catholic connection. Of course, Ireland had a climate that conditioned and compelled religious choices, but what could get forgotten was the flexibility and democratic variety of born-again Christianity which, despite America's fundamentalist television evangelists, depends on personal interpretation of the Bible – a far cry from Catholicism, which dictates dogma through an authoritarian hierarchy.

Sociologically, the Lypton Village conversion was fascinating. Ex-Catholics like myself, Geldof or Paul McGuinness, who'd been force-fed the Catechism at school, passed on spiritual exploration. For us, Catholicism and therefore religion was a bar to personal development. But U2, students of Ireland's first multi-denominational comprehensive, schooling that was anathema to Ireland's Catholic hierarchy, lacked those inhibitions. They even showed originality and foresight. The hippie Eastern sects had been discredited as lazy and ludicrous cultural aberrations. U2,

at least, would choose a path in tune with their culture.

They joined the Shalom Bible group whose leader, Chris Rowe, was the son of a missionary who'd ministered alongside the Olympic hero and inspiration of *Chariots of Fire* Eric Liddell in China. Rowe had been a charismatic and in the context of born again Christianity, Shalom was as much Pentecostalist as fundamentalist, and committed to the surrender of the ego before the healing grace and fiery breath of the Holy Ghost. Though it was rarely couched in specifically Christian terms, this theme of self-surrender would continually resurface in U2's early albums.

In Dublin, the rumours continued about the Shalom Bible group, that Lypton Village had joined. Tales circulated about collective confessions and truth sessions at Shalom's premises off Capel Street just north of the Liffey. Not all Lypton Village were discreet about their beliefs. Some proselytized, causing a mixture of annoyance and amusement within the scene.

Lypton Village were a fine catch for Shalom, glamorizing fundamentalism's previously dour image. But Shalom soon lost Gavin Friday. With his girlfriend Renee – significantly both of them conventionally schooled outside Mount Temple – he was the first to depart. Gradually the Prunes left Shalom except their drummer, Pod (Anthony Murphy). Caught between his beliefs and the band, he finally quit the Prunes to join U2's roadcrew.

These differences only became chronic after U2 signed to Island. They never led to any irretrievable breakdown of relationships. It wasn't in both their tolerant natures for the Edge and Dik, the Evan's brothers, to fall out, while Gavin agreed to differ with Bono. Eventually Christianity would seem to function for U2 as an early shield against the potential corruptions of the road, serving to intensify their will in their years of campaigning outside Ireland.

I've also often speculated if Christianity may have been a special shield for Bono. As the focus of the audience's apathy or acclaim, front men always have the most vulnerable and volatile egos. But imbued with a missionary sense – however unfocused – and believing his gift came from above, Bono may have been protected from

Larry at a Lypton Village party
Behind the drums, confident and in his element

those identity and ego problems that can upset those singers who find their fame has neither savour nor reason.

Bono's confession didn't reduce my appreciation of U2. I might diverge from their doctrines but I couldn't deny their artistic spirit. Their beliefs hadn't made their music some vacant and lamely trendy folk Mass. I quieted any personal doubts by speculating whether U2's combining of religion with rock owed more to American than British models.

But Bob Dylan hadn't yet announced his controversial conversion in 'Slow Train Coming'. The Village didn't listen to Little Richard or Jerry Lee Lewis and so didn't know how Dixie fundamentalism was interwoven with rock 'n' roll. Black singers weren't on their turntables either; the commerce between gospel and soul was also unknown to them. Yet U2 had somehow stumbled upon a course other Europeans had previously studiously ignored. Out of an apparently conservative belief-system, they had actually produced an artistic conundrum.

Adding to the enigma was Adam's refusal to align himself with Shalom while the other three participated with varying degrees of fervour. The Edge's beliefs seemed most lightly and carefully held; some observers would suggest that it was his girlfriend, and later wife, Aislinn, who was more involved. Certainly Bono and Larry were more intense than he was.

For the drummer, 1979 was a traumatic year of decision on many fronts. Their prosperous family backgrounds had given Adam and the Edge social *savoir-faire* and confidence, while Bono could always bluff. But if Larry could be a most critical contributor to the band's post mortems after each show, the most typically Irish teenager in U2 was then the shyest in public.

He was also the most cautious. The only member with a day job, he was often last to soundchecks and a problem at rehearsals, sometimes slotting in his drums after the others had sketched out the music, entirely the reverse of requirements. Nobody doubted his ability, but the band and especially Paul McGuinness worried about his commitment. They vaguely considered easing him out. Steve Averill was consulted about any available replacements; another drummer and

sometime roadie for the band, Eric Briggs even sat in on a few rehearsals.

Then Larry's mother died. Shalom became a support in Larry's grief. Bono, who had earlier been devastated by the loss of his mother, Iris, became his intimate. Leaving his job as a messenger boy, Larry threw all his energies into the band. His place in U2 had ceased to be an issue.

The band's growing Dublin audience knew nothing of these traumas. They just thought U2 the most colourful and energetic noise in town. Despite their beliefs, U2 were positive, welcoming and without any repellent cultishness. As for the band themselves, they decided that now was the time to get attention outside Ireland and start the campaign to capture that elusive recording deal.

They thought the first opportunity had come in February when the Project Arts Centre hosted 'Dark Space', a multi-media weekend all-nighter. Rudi, then the latest Northern hopeful with their single "Big Time", came from Belfast with Terri Hooley and the Good Vibrations gang. Public Image, Throbbing Gristle and the Mekons were invited from the UK, though eventually only the latter played. The event was also meant to be a platform for the other new Dublin bands emerging alongside U2 and the Prunes.

The Blades, led by Paul Cleary, knit the influences of the Jam and Elvis Costello with stinging harmonies and the scene's most danceable rhythm section. D.C. Nien were a raw relative of Ultravox whose bludgeoning rhythmic power wasn't always matched with compensating melodic grace. Slightly older than the rest, The Atrix were a jerky keyboard group, sometimes derivative of XTC, yet capable of a stridently moody Continental circus atmosphere at their best.

Dublin believed itself isolated. Throughout '78, the London music weeklies had been discovering and promoting vibrant post-punk scenes in almost every provincial British city. Bristol, Sheffield, Leeds, Liverpool, Manchester and Edinburgh had all been hailed as centres of the new renaissance. In late '78 Stiff Little Fingers and the Undertones had brought Northern Ireland to the fore. Surely now it was Dublin's turn, especially since a *New Musical Express* writer was accompanying the Mekons. Furthermore, the BBC's own Arts

Council for every aspiring garage-band, disc-jockey John Peel, was travelling down with the Good Vibrations mob.

Expectations were not fulfilled. U2 played a glittering set, but the eventual *NME* feature devoted its page-and-a-half to the Mekons with hardly a paragraph on the event. As for John Peel, suffering from a throat complaint, he was speechless for medical not musical reasons. But U2 were too effusive, too overbearing for his taste. They would be one of the very few young bands of the era that didn't benefit from his endorsement.

It was easy to get despondent, to be defensive and oversensitive, to feel that the London insiders regarded Dubliners as second-class citizens. U2 could only keep grafting as Paul McGuinness began his rounds of the London record companies with the first official demo, produced by Horslips bassist Barry Devlin.

London not Dublin was where decisions were made. Traditionally distribution and marketing organizations with little informed interest in native talent, the Irish subsidiaries of the record companies had even less influence with their London head offices. Managers like Paul McGuinness couldn't pause to complain about cultural neo-colonialism; they had no option but to bypass Dublin.

Still, there was one partial exception, CBS Ireland, the most successful local company of the late seventies where U2 had an early ally in Jackie Hayden. Hayden and his boss, David Duke, had sunk some of their profits into home releases though the beneficiaries were usually MOR acts. Besides, the policy was partially a PR exercise to prove that CBS weren't just another uncaring, greedy multinational company repatriating all their profits out of Ireland.

Hayden himself was more alert to the new Irish talent than his contemporaries in the other Dublin companies. Outside of CBS, his own cottage label, Midnite, had worked with Steve Averill and Phil Chevron of the Radiators. He had also tried and failed to interest CBS in the Boomtown Rats. Very soon after the Limerick contest, he offered U2 a deal.

The standard Irish contract then was grossly unbalanced. U2 got the promise of two or three singles whereas CBS got world rights, potentially for five years. Even before the arrival of Paul McGuinness, U2 knew the offer was premature. They consulted unofficial advisers like myself, calmly quizzed Hayden, and then politely refused his offer. They were too young, they agreed, they needed time to develop. Besides, Larry and the Edge weren't yet eighteen. As minors, their signatures might not be binding.

Hayden wasn't annoyed by their rebuff. Instead he was impressed by how sensibly and diplomatically these teenagers had handled his offer. Other Irish acts would either have bawled him out or naively signed any contract. Hayden kept in touch and began mentioning U2 in his regular reports to Nicky Graham in CBS London's A & R department.

Independently Paul McGuinness had interested a CBS scout, Chas De Whalley, a former *Sounds* writer, who flew to Dublin to view U2. Ten years later, De Whalley recalls that it was Bono who first impressed him. Was he exaggerating when he saw Bono as a future David Bowie? Perhaps, but in a lesser commercial league U2's singer had the same theatrical qualities as the Scottish maverick Alex Harvey. Obviously Bono's sessions with Mannix Flynn and Conal Kearney were paying off.

So De Whalley got to produce U2's next set of demos. But he gave them grief and lip and Bono was tempted to punch out this rather superior Englishman. Besides, Chas had problems with their rhythm section. In London A & R circles, New York's Chic, sublimely marrying disco and funk had become a most influential sound as producers tightened up rhythm sections for the disco floor. But Adam and Larry on bass and drums were hardly Chic's Bernard Edwards and Tony Thompson.

U2 hardly listened to Black music, only Joy Division's meddling with disco might have touched them. For De Whalley, Larry was powerful but overplaying, possibly due to his father's jazz tastes, while Adam was as much relating to the Edge's harmonics as connecting with the drummer. Neither was anchoring U2 to his satisfaction.

He still believed in their potential, however. Jackie Hayden was also pressurizing CBS London, but neither could persuade their superiors. Regularly Chas would troop over to Dublin with a senior

CBS executive. Equally regularly U2 would choose that night to play an off-colour set with Bono's exuberance curdling into shrill desperation, and De Whalley's superior would leave unconvinced.

So a stand-off was agreed and CBS London let De Whalley's sessions be released as U2's debut Irish single, 'U2:Three', consisting of 'Out of Control', 'Stories For Boys' and 'Boy/Girl'. This new deal was a neat trade-off, unprecedented at that time in Ireland. U2 got a launch pad release but Paul McGuinness was still free to negotiate abroad. In return for this early gesture of support, CBS Ireland had U2 for the small home market for the next five years. Should U2 be eventually successful through another London company, CBS profited without any future production costs of its own.

Still, CBS had to mount a decent opening promotional campaign. 'U2:Three' was the first Irish twelve-inch with a thousand individual numbered copies, which have now made it a collector's item, though Jackie Hayden suspects there have since been many more forged versions in American circulation. Listeners to Dave Fanning's radio show were polled to choose 'Out of Control' as the A-side, and Steve Averill and Hugo McGuinness were employed to design the sleeve.

Adam took the most interest in their image. He wanted a look like 'a modern sixties band' that again wouldn't tie U2 to any tribe. Bono regularly spoke of U2's classic line-up employing 'the primary colours' of rock, so U2 relied on black, white and red for their designs, a policy which with the exception of the 'October' sleeve, they have consistently followed to this day. So for an early publicity shot, they decided Bono should wear white with the others in black. Ever thorough, the band arrived at the photo session with six full suitcases of borrowed clothes.

They weren't always so accommodating. Hugo needed Bono's lyrics for inspiration but the singer became mysteriously unavailable when the photographer went searching for them. Once Bono even darted down a side alley when he saw Hugo approaching him on Grafton Street. A fortnight later, Bono's elusive behaviour was explained. He didn't have any final set of lyrics, he was

A guitar made by Dik, the Edge's brother, smashed on stage by Dave Id during a Virgin Prunes concert and rescued by Adam

improvising them on stage. Then at another photo session, Steve had to hide Larry's feet: the least fashion-conscious member of U2 had arrived in … flares!

U2 already knew both their direction and destination. In autumn '79, they had worked out both the essential concept and image of the *Boy* album that would only be released a year later. They would stress innocence and Hugo McGuinness had already shot the photographs using Peter Rowan, the younger brother of Derek (Guggi in the Prunes) as the central icon for the sleeve.

Meanwhile 'U2: Three' justified Jackie Hayden's confidence in the band. The thousand twelve inches were quickly snapped up and the conventional seven inch sold equally well, an excellent debut in a country of three million which was still under the shadow of the showbands.

But in Dublin, U2 were now encountering a resistance that sometimes flared into open enmity. It wasn't just the envy and backbiting that all young bands can encounter among their contemporaries. Between U2 and their detractors, there was a major rift in values. The band just didn't conform to the black-leather-jacketed tradition of rebellion that led from Keith Richards to Johnny Thunders and the Clash. Was this honest originality, or a commercial sell-out manipulated by Paul McGuinness? U2's critics preferred to believe the latter.

Besides Bono's unquenchable eagerness to communicate, his refusal and inability to be studied and aloof made him an obvious target to taunt. Later the guitarist with the Stars of Heaven, Stan Erraught was both a Modern Heirs member and a Trinity student in '79 when U2 played there. He and a friend wandered to the front of the stage and teased Bono, tipping at the microphone to knock him off his cues. Somehow – Stan can't remember how – the joke went sour: Bono leapt off the stage and wrestled Stan's friend to the floor. Another time, another place: now the guy who nettled Bono works in America for Ireland's leading insurance company.

Less trivial was a controversy that erupted in the lively and highly opinionated Dublin fanzine *Heat*. Its editors, Pete Price and Jude Carr couldn't abide U2. For instance one night at McGonagle's, Jude had

mocked the band, accusing them of being a clone of Billy Idol's glam-pop variation on punk, Generation X. Now *Heat* printed a story alleging sharp practice by Paul McGuinness.

In May '79 Joe Jackson had been booked to make his Irish debut at Trinity College with another Dublin band, Rocky De Valera and the Gravediggers as support. But, claimed *Heat*, someone had made a fraudulent phone-call pretending to be a London A & M executive who wanted the Gravediggers dumped and replaced by U2 so he could see this promising new Irish band.

As it happened, the Gravediggers did support Jackson. And nobody could ever discover who made the call if indeed it had ever been made. Certainly it hadn't emanated from Paul McGuinness who was coldly furious about this slur on the good name he treasured. He immediately organized a solicitor's letter to *Heat*, demanding the magazine's withdrawal. But its distributors, Eason's, failed to call in every offending copy. McGuinness renewed his legal campaign and *Heat* was liquidated.

Later Carr and Price claimed that anyway, they had been looking for a suitably colourful excuse to close down *Heat* since it had become too much hard labour. They celebrated its controversial demise with a benefit party. If this local spat didn't really damage U2 with their own fans, it certainly further soured the atmosphere between the band and Dublin's punk purists.

More threatening were the Black Catholics, a gang from Bono's own Cedarwood Road neighbourhood. With their motto, 'Young, Drunk and Proud', they fancied themselves as the scene's leading hardmen and their main mission in '79 seemed to consist of disruptive stage invasions – Squeeze and the Revillos were two victims – and insulting U2.

The band were hardly so successful to inspire such animosity. After all 'U2: Three' wasn't even released till September. Yet they remained the target of resentment for innumerable ill-considered reasons. You just weren't allowed to be both ambitious and middle-class, that second charge particularly infuriating Bono since he saw little difference in the public service employment of his father and theirs.

Nonetheless, the Black Catholics decided U2 were 'Prods', stuck-up

Hugo's first publicity photo session with the band. Adam felt they should try to produce a modern sixties look using black-and-white colours only. Bono suggested for the session that he wear white and the band wear black. This way the singer was always defined without having to be upfront in photographs. It was also Bono who suggested putting Larry to the fore of the photographs. To this day they continue to use black and white with a dash of red for album covers, posters and so on

'Protestant bastards'. The first reckoning came in September when the band supported punk troubadour, Patrick Fitzgerald for two nights at the Project Arts Centre. Cider was flung at Adam. About twenty punks threatened an invasion as Bono took off his shoe to ward them off the low stage before they were evicted. The next night, a group of the Black Catholics appeared, drunk after a cider party. They would claim they intended no disruption but at the first hint of trouble, the reinforced Project security were in no mood to be conciliatory. They ejected the gang after a bruising tussle in the foyer with Paul McGuinness to the fore, dragging out one of the offenders by the hair. It was hardly Altamont – the Black Catholics were more mouth than muscle – but don't ever believe the young U2 were unanimously hailed in Dublin.

The feud continued. Another night after a row at the party of a punkette who knew both the Black Catholics and Lypton Village factions, Guggi's van was wrecked. Then, at the Baggot Inn, a Black Catholic threw beer glasses at the band and was frog-marched out. Bono's patience was at an end. Totally steamed up, he marched down Cedarwood Road to the offender's house and confronted his father. All round the neighbourhood he went looking for his antagonist. Finally he faced him down and by Bono's account, his opponent cut and ran. Whatever, the Black Catholics didn't trouble U2 again.

Still, they had their own milder, puckish ways of winding up the scene. Once they sent Hugo McGuinness and an American friend, Pat McAllister, with a filmless camera to the Bailey to pose as a *Rolling Stone* team researching a major feature on the Dublin music scene, a hoax that all that bar's would-be stars totally fell for.

But U2 were rarely seen propping up the bar of the Bailey. Their priority was chiselling away in a rehearsal room 'sculpting' their sound in the Edge's words. It was this dedication that had led to 'U2:Three' which they intended as their London calling card. At EMI Tom Nolan heard it. Half-Irish, he obviously had extra reasons to be sympathetic. Also impressed by a *Sounds* article by Dave McCullough championing them, he visited Dublin to see U2 at the Dandelion and returned to London speaking in tongues.

His EMI superiors came to see U2 at the Baggot Inn. This was intended to be the triumphant night. Besides EMI, there was a scout from Stiff plus Muff Winwood from CBS, representing their continuing if sceptical interest. Nobody in the U2 camp now recalls it as one of those erratic nights that might have merited a thumbs-down. When U2 left the stage, they confidently expected someone would offer them a contract.

Instead their hopes were dashed. The most experienced observer, Muff Winwood, once bassist with the Spencer Davis group, told Paul McGuinness he still couldn't see Larry Mullen as a time-keeper. He'd have to go or shape up before Winwood could make any positive recommendation.

At least Winwood was courteous, but the EMI executives didn't even bother to talk to Paul McGuinness. They left early to watch the Specials on television, a band Tom Nolan had already failed to interest EMI in. Back in London, Nolan was asked to apologize for wasting their time on a wild goose chase. Later he would be sacked in EMI cutbacks. To this day, Tom Nolan believes his support of U2 was the black mark that led to his firing. Meanwhile EMI follow a policy of chequebook A & R, expensively signing all the British acts they missed first time around, playing the transfer market like Manchester United, and just as successfully.

At CBS, Jackie Hayden and Chas De Whalley still fought U2's corner. In a final throw, De Whalley supervised a London demo session that became their second CBS Ireland single, 'Another Day'. For U2, it was a failed and mistaken attempt to emulate the Jam as a singles band. Bono's voice was shot from performing the previous night and he spent the whole day drinking lemon and honey medications. Nobody recalls it as a triumph and CBS remained unconvinced. De Whalley was promoted to be product manager on the CBS sister label, Epic, and then quit, frustrated by CBS's refusal to sign U2 and by the company's reluctance to support other recent British signings.

A & M's Charlie Eyre was the next scout to be spurned. On his first Dublin mission, he checked U2 and now admits he hated them. On a return visit to see the

Bono holds his shoe in his hand ready to ward off a stage invasion when playing support to Patrick Fitzgerald in the Project Arts Centre. Hugo took this shot just before a bottle was smashed over his back: luckily, he was protected by his leather jacket. Phil Chevron from The Radiators, who had been deeply affected by the death of a fan at their University College Dublin concert, spent an hour in the dressing-room after the gig consoling the band

Advance Records in South King Street.
The only record shop in Dublin to stock independent record labels and a mecca for Dublin's punks and Black catholics.

Blades play an early evening set, he asked A & M's Dublin rep, John Buckley, who was playing late night. Only U2, said Buckley, who persuaded a highly reluctant Eyre to take a second look. Of course, U2 tore down McGonagle's, Eyre was converted and immediately invited the band and McGuinness to his hotel to plot an A & M signing.

Since Eyre presented A & M as a company that would take a long-term view, McGuinness was interested. Eyre and a senior A & M executive flew to Dublin to see U2, again at McGonagle's. But technically things went awry, the band played a disjointed set and that was the end of any beautiful friendship between U2 and A & M.

Still, there was a generous footnote. After signing to Island, U2 were in London rehearsing one afternoon at the Lyceum. Eyre's girlfriend, passing by, recognized the U2 sound and slipped in to observe them from the back of the stalls. Bono noticed the lone observer and started questioning her. How did she know U2? Through my boyfriend. And who was he? Oh, Charlie Eyre. Whereupon he set up a chair and table at the front of the hall and U2 played their full set for her.

But autumn '79 was a fraught time for U2 and Paul McGuinness. They'd set out their stall and seemingly exhausted all possible outlets. What had gone wrong?

It wasn't Larry Mullen's drumming but a different musical problem. In Dublin, U2 might promote themselves as a youthful pop band, but it was total experience of a U2 set that counted – Bono's gymnastics and his conviction as he played the Fool, the surges of their dynamics as the songs blended into a unique adolescent rock symphony. Once inside the music, you got emotionally enveloped and attuned to its codes, but the London spies came cold, looked for The Hit, and found U2 gauche and formless on a bad night.

Again if you knew U2, you also knew how Bono's hypersensitivity was linked to their volatility. He had to connect, he had to improvise some new gesture each night, he had to risk making mistakes, he lacked the experience to then cover and correct. Sometimes his instincts were uncanny like that Dandelion coup that converted Hugo McGuinness. But when he failed to channel the energy in the hall, his unchecked

My brains hurt. Bono in pensive mood

emotionalism often led to embarrassment, grieving and much collective gnashing of teeth in the dressing room afterwards.

To be fair to the A & R visitors, U2 were a conundrum. They were inclusive whereas punk could be exclusive. Punk meant reinventing oneself in a superior, private world, whereas Bono was unashamedly public, someone who would prefer to risk appearing sentimental rather than being cynical. He just didn't have that suspicious shield, that defensive armour of attitude against the world!

Moreover, though U2 were young, obviously influenced by New Wave guitar bands like Television and the Only Ones, and with no likeness to elder lemons like Yes, Genesis or Led Zeppelin, where were the singles? Punk wasn't only artistically revitalized British pop; its emphasis on the single had also given the UK companies a quick return on their investments. U2 offered no instant profit – another reason for CBS's lack of interest in them.

Paul McGuinness wouldn't be fobbed off by singles or short-term album deals. He never wanted his band to be at the mercy of record companies whose senior executives, and thus company policies, changed with the seasons. In Ireland, U2 were already proving they could find their audience and deliver record sales. Therefore, Paul McGuinness argued, U2 should deliver the finished records without company interference.

It was also increasingly apparent that U2 were pre-eminently a live band. They could only succeed through tireless touring that would be dependent on generous record company support. There was simply no sense in entering any marriage of convenience that was fated to eventual and ignoble divorce, probably on the initiative of a company that would misunderstand and meddle with U2. Ironically it would be the non-punk U2 who would most insist upon and eventually achieve the Clash's demand for 'complete control'.

Paul McGuinness's own personality just wouldn't have allowed him to take any inferior role, wheedling for favours as the junior manager of just another supplicant act on a major label's extensive roster. Yet what McGuinness sought wasn't unprecedented, even for an act as youthful as U2. But such contracts were generally only awarded to experienced managers, not to an Irish unknown with neither industry contacts nor a previous track record.

In Dublin, heads were shaken at his rejection of the conventional wisdom. His single-mindedness was deemed irresponsible and inexcusable stubbornness. He was so unrealistic, he was being thrown out of record companies. That was the claim made by the manager of another Dublin band, who'd just negotiated a deal that would collapse, with his clients being dropped eighteen months after their signing.

Yet in Autumn '79, those arguments were supportable. To onlookers, U2 seemed stymied. Worse, they almost lost Edge. His parents had allowed him a sabbatical year to devote to the band. But now those twelve months were over and the guitarist had to deliver his side of the family bargain and go and study engineering at Bolton Street Technical College.

Hugo McGuinness recalls one lunchtime scene in Trinity's Buttery where Bono and Adam plotted to steal Edge's application forms. They failed, but the Edge's heart obviously wasn't in the engineering course. One evening at a band meeting in Paul McGuinness's house, the other three happened on his copy-book. The first page was meticulously ruled out with the lecture notes equally minutely entered. But on the next page, the ruling straggled across the page and there were band notes beneath the engineering entries. On the third page, there was only a doodle of an amp. It was obvious where the Edge's loyalties lay!

He was crucial to the band's sound. Outsiders would later suggest his habit of repeating and varying phrases owed a debt to Irish traditional music. True, there was a Celtic connection in his father's membership of Dublin's Welsh male voice choir and you could arguably detect a jig-like lilt – somewhere between Thin Lizzy and the Horslips – on 'A Day Without Me', their second Island single. But there were few Irish folk records in the Evans' household record collection. You could more easily argue the Edge's use of subtle repetitions came from an early interest in the records of Brian Eno of whom he was a fan long before that innovator produced *The Unforgettable Fire*.

He was already experimenting with

The Edge, a keen amateur photographer, in between takes readjusts the lights to take his own shots

echo units. Paul McGuinness didn't immediately understand when the band asked him to find a 'Memoryman' effect. Surely, he argued, Edge wanted to be a proper guitarist? Proper guitarists didn't need to fiddle with echo. But the band won the argument; they knew their artistic priorities.

But after the Baggot disaster, U2 had to find another avenue by which to attract new record company attention. They were holding and expanding their Dublin audience which would continue its loyal support but that was insufficient in itself. If the London record companies were apathetic, U2 would now look to the British music press to promote their case.

In '79, *Q* and *The Face* didn't exist. *New Musical Express, Melody Maker, Sounds* and *Record Mirror* sold double what they sell now. In line with punk's change of personnel, the four weeklies had recruited a new generation of writers from the fanzines, who professed to be the audience's own fervent and often vituperative tribunes. Their support could be more influential than that of any A & R scout, their praise of any hopeful guaranteeing a veritable squad of company reps at their next date.

Bono had already made the initiative on this front. As far back as April, he'd visited London to hustle both press and the record companies, accompanied by Andrew Whiteway, a Trinity student who spent a year as the band's tour manager, their costs

Adam with his original Rikenbacker bass. The only bass player in Dublin with one. He bought the guitar because he thought it was a cool one to have, but once he started to master his technique he swiftly changed over to a Fender which he still uses today

partially defrayed by Bono's assignment to review Thin Lizzy and Iggy Pop for *Hot Press*. The expedition had its naff moments. Visiting the basement office of publicist Tony Brainsby to get their Thin Lizzy tickets, Bono confidently marched down its staircase, tripped on the Cuban heels of his boots and pitched full and fast forward onto the carpet of London's most prestigious music PR company. Ringing up John Peel, he frantically jammed his silver into an unreliable coinbox on a faulty line. Peel continued to be unimpressed by U2.

More useful was Bono's visit to the Covent Garden offices of *Sounds* and its companion paper *Record Mirror*, where Dave McCullough and Chris Westwood shared a desk. For the next year, the pair would be U2's most effective sponsors.

A Belfastman, McCullough had co-edited that city's fanzine, *Alternative Ulster* with Gavin Martin, later of *NME*. Argumentative, his punk pseudonym had been Dave Angry. Almost puritanical in his scorn for industry waste, often close to proprietorial in his view of a band, and sufficiently intense and idealistic to be regularly disillusioned by any band he might have championed, McCullough scorned falsity and was soon taken by Bono's mixture of principle and quicksilver charm.

Bono and the way he'd look and talk at you. Adam might be U2's good natured envoy to the business, but Bono was already becoming the band's most engaging and fluent spokesman to the media. It wasn't just that he was a journalist's dream as an unstoppable talker. Rather, as the stories unfolded, he had the ability to persuade the interviewer that U2 were his own private discovery and that the journalist had been cast by the fates to play his own absolutely personalized role in U2's crusade against the forces of darkness.

September saw McCullough in Dublin preparing a centrespread feature that headlined U2 but also included the Virgin Prunes, the Blades, D.C. Nien and The Atrix. Hugo McGuinness met a McCullough surprised by the numbers crushed into the Baggot. He didn't realize U2 had so many fans. Well, actually, said Hugo, partially exaggerating, half of them hate U2, they're here for you, Dave! You're almost as popular as the Pope!

This was true. McCullough's article

legitimized the isolated Dublin scene in its own eyes. U2 were *real*. The other bands were *real*. Therefore the scene was *real* now McCullough had given the London stamp of approval. And inspecting U2, he focused on Bono's absorbing stage presence. When a mike broke, 'instead of panicking, he used the fluke, calling a kid from the audience down front, thrusting the mike into his upheld right hand and using his right arm, as it were, as a mike stand throughout the song'.

Next *Record Mirror* and Chris Westwood would give U2 their first cover story outside Ireland. In November, Rough Trade released 'U2: Three' in Britain and U2 decided to go to London to capture an English audience and prove their Irish success was no Celtic freak.

'The most evocative, romantic new rockpop band since the heyday Penetration and The Buzzcocks', wrote Westwood about this 'breath of fresh Eire' perceptively noting that what distinguished U2 and made them 'so believable is their awareness of vulnerability, both in themselves and in other individuals. They see acceptance of this as central to the very concept of harmony, unity and self-belief.'

'Dublin's in a constant state of amber,' Bono told Westwood in an image that perfectly crystallized Ireland's lazily repressive, arbitrary tolerance and their own impatience at the roadblocks in the London record companies. But unbeknownst to Bono, the amber light was soon to finally switch to green; Island Records were starting to check out U2.

Island hadn't really figured in Paul McGuinness's previous rounds. Though the most resourceful rock independent through the first half of the seventies, the company was going through a period of retrenchment. Overreliant on Bob Marley, Island had lost acts like Roxy Music and Bad Company which it had nursed to stardom. Besides, Island had sat out punk – its two leading hopes having been the faltering pre-punks Eddie and the Hot Rods and the first edition of Ultravox, who would only sell when they moved to Chrysalis and Midge Ure replaced John Foxx as their singer and prime songwriter.

Later all concerned at Island would agree that the company wasn't consciously seeking a new young band. Nonetheless U2

The Edge playing his Gibson Explorer. A bargain buy in America when he was on holiday with the family. It was the first in Ireland and the envy of many Dublin musicians

did conveniently fill a gap in the company's roster. In particular, their American distributors, Warner, would be thankful that Island had finally signed a genuine rock quartet that could be promoted with conviction in the US market.

Island's A & R head was then Bill Stewart. An entirely untypical figure in the music business as an Old Harrovian and MCC member who later played cricket against Ireland, Stewart had been recruited from advertising by Island's managing director, Martin Davis. Nicknamed 'The Captain', Stewart had previously served in the British army, including a tour of duty as a community officer in Derry, where he'd witnessed the Undertones in their earliest days.

But the credit for signing U2 equally belongs to Island's chief press officer, Rob Partridge who'd been alerted by the effusive coverage the band were receiving through *Hot Press*, McCullough and Westwood. A droll west countryman and former *Melody Maker* writer, Rob Partridge would emerge as an increasingly influential personality at Island, later becoming a director and taking control of the in-house jazz and minority music label Antilles that launched Courtney Pine. And, once Paul McGuinness recognized Island's interest, he as much courted the company through the press office as through their A & R department, pestering Partridge with his phone-calls.

Partridge and Stewart had heard 'U2:Three' but neither had seen the band till they played London in December '79. The tour almost didn't happen. Paul McGuinness was negotiating a publishing deal that would subsidize the dates. At the last moment, the publishing company Bryan Morrison Music added new conditions. McGuinness thought these insupportable and despite the potential damage, the manager coldly withdrew. Friends and family bankrolled the London tour.

It worked. The half-dozen club dates won U2 their first London loyalists. For *Hot Press*, Ross Fitzsimons saw them at the Moonlight Club, supporting the Dolly Mixtures before a meagre audience. What impressed Fitzsimons was again how Bono's fresh approach contrasted with usual London strategies as when he 'went to take off his sweater, he handed the mike to the nearest punter to hold for him. The guy's

bewilderment turned to amazement to laughter as Bono … thanked him for his help … rock singers don't *do* that sort of thing.' Fitzsimons also saw them at the Lyceum, on trial as bottom of the bill to Talking Heads and Orchestral Manoeuvres in the Dark when again, they got a creditable reception.

More significantly, Stewart and Partridge were also impressed. But the Christmas season prevented any business activity. The next episode didn't happen until U2 toured Ireland in February '80. Myth now has it that this tour was a despairing last throw by a financially beleaguered Paul McGuinness. The legend is only partially true. McGuinness *was* stretched because as U2 were building, expenses were exceeding income at each stage. Besides, with no other companies competing with Island, he couldn't orchestrate an auction for the perfect deal. But U2 retained press support and had the momentum to increase both their Irish and London audiences. They could probably have gained some indie deal through Rough Trade or a similar label but for Paul McGuinness, that would have been a climbdown that didn't guarantee future security.

Moreover, the idea of playing Dublin's National Stadium was conceived by the band's Irish agent, Dave Kavanagh. McGuinness thought it premature. He was only persuaded when that January, U2 won five categories in the *Hot Press* readers' poll, beating out established Irish favourites like Thin Lizzy and the Boomtown Rats.

The victory was a morale boost but U2 almost didn't survive the tour. The Republic of Ireland doesn't have motorways. Driving back at night along unlit, twisting roads can be a gruelling exercise in concentration. Returning from Sligo in the west of Ireland in the band's van, Dave Kavanagh's mind went automatic and he almost fell into a doze till an alert Adam Clayton poked him awake. They wouldn't have been the first Irish music casualty on Ireland's highways.

Meanwhile at Island, Bill Stewart was now convinced. But though he had Rob Partridge's support, the other senior Island executives wouldn't unconditionally accept the unconventional newcomer's judgement. Stewart's deputy, Annie Roseberry and two executives from Island's publishing arm, Blue Mountain, were despatched to Belfast

An example of U2's willingness to
experiment and make mistakes. These
early concepts for publicity shots just
didn't work

for a final examination.

The team's responses were mixed. The Blue Mountain duo were unimpressed, but Annie Roseberry loved them. Stewart and Partridge had already identified the Edge as a special guitarist but Annie Roseberry was refreshed by the band's generosity. It became a giddy night. The band and Annie drove back to the Europa Hotel with Adam jammed in the boot of the car and were stopped by the British army. Later, when the increasingly exuberant bassist spilled his drink all over her, Annie recalls a solicitous Paul McGuinness, obviously alarmed the deal might evaporate just like the alcohol splattered all over her clothes.

They continued celebrating. U2 have a reputation for civil conduct as a band who don't trash hotel rooms. But that night they did. The room keys beside Paul McGuinness were left unguarded on the bar. They took them and trooped upstairs, re arranged the room, smeared shaving-cream on the mirror and returned to the bar, smirking in triumph as they replaced the keys on the counter beside their unsuspecting manager. But, when another resident picked up the keys, they soon learned that McGuinness had absolutely no reason to suspect or worry. Their extravagance was in vain, U2 had wrecked an innocent resident's room.

But if that hotel resident was confused, U2 weren't: Bono's 'constant state of amber' was over. U2's constant state of amber was over. Annie Roseberry flew back to London to give the green light for go. So Bill Stewart was empowered to fly to Dublin, enter U2's dressing room at the National Stadium and finally offer them that elusive recording contract.

But no story can ever end quite so neatly. U2 had one further audition for Island when they returned to London on March 19 to feature in the 'Sense of Ireland' festival and were inspected by other senior Island executives. The show at the Acklam Hall was easy to sell since U2 had just been the subject of a glowing *NME* cover story by Paul Morley who'd also suffered painful rural Irish culture-shock watching U2 play alongside an Irish showband in Tipperary. Morley's tribute strengthened the hand of Paul McGuinness as did their intense Acklam Hall show which proved to Island, U2 could be much more than local Irish heroes.

Four days later, on March 23, the spring equinox, the documents were actually signed in, of all incongruous places, the ladies toilet of the Lyceum. U2's talent and toil had been finally justified.

Only one last point remains to be clarified. U2 were an Island (UK) signing; the company's founder and owner, Chris Blackwell, was not involved. He only entered the plot when he saw them playing in London, later that summer. Once Blackwell was converted that night, American doors would start to swing open for U2.

But that's the next chapter in their story, though of course, you can argue that U2's real artistic history only began when they signed to Island. Yet if U2's first two years in Ireland showed scant recording reward – 'U2:Three' and 'Another Day' though now collector's items, can only be regarded as juvenilia – their Irish apprenticeship gave U2 an identity that would essentially last until *The Unforgettable Fire*. Perhaps acts from rock's badlands need to be harder than the rest. Certainly Bruce Springsteen from New Jersey and Prince from Minnesota share with U2 the single-mindedness and sense of perspective that

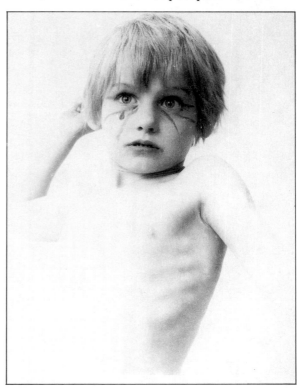

top: U2 in their first headline gig outside Dublin in the Arcadia in Cork. Over two thousand turned up to see four Dublin bands, but by the time U2 took to the stage after midnight only two hundred people remained
bottom: U2 play Queen's University Belfast: in the audience are Annie Roseberry from Island and her two colleagues from Blue Mountain

distance from the musical metropolitan centres of London, Los Angeles and New York can give. To both survive and create, outsiders need to know who they are very early on.

I can't now put my hand on my heart and say I predicted or even expected that they would become *Rolling Stone's* 'Band Of The Eighties' or make the cover of *Time*. But I did know they rarely made mean or stupid mistakes. I did know that Paul McGuinness's original 'Baby Band' – a concept they soon forced him to drop – never ran before they walked and rarely ever fell before the next step. Those early Dublin days had revealed their intrinsic character. I was certain that as long as U2 retained their collective purpose, they would never falter in their chosen endeavours. U2's Irish isolation had put sufficient iron in their soul.

Their Irish isolation had other artistic consequences. In a 1958 essay on the Irish painter, Jack Yeats, the English art critic, John Berger wrote: 'Ireland has not yet reached that critical point where she can only defend her way of life: she is still striving, staggering, suffering and dreaming her way towards one … it is impossible to appreciate Yeats without understanding something of this.'

I strongly suspect U2 would recoil from any exact comparisons with W.B.'s brother. Yet like many Irish artists, a similar spirit pervades U2, though their Irish romanticism preferred the artistic construction of a community to the political destruction of one. Besides, for U2, rock was still a young and beguilingly innocent art form. They could still imagine it as something life-giving, a positive value to contrast against the sterile culture of the showbands. In time, they would pal with rock veterans like Pete Townshend. A generation separated them but not the experience of living in a place and time where rock was changing a culture.

This experience also gave them their ambiguous attitude towards punk. Beyond Ireland in the immediate aftermath of punk, artistry in rock often consisted of fracturing reality but rarely reconstructing its fragments. In contrast, U2 dared to transcend reality. After all, wasn't being in an Irish band in the seventies, especially with their ambition, itself unreal? Or in

John Berger's phrase, 'striving, staggering, suffering and dreaming' towards some new life?

This urge to transcendence could lead to much misunderstanding. John Berger, again from the Jack Yeats essay: 'Further, it is Yeats' Irish background which explains why his direct influence on younger European painters would be a dangerous one, leading to theatrical mannerism.'

Likewise with U2 and especially their lightning-conductor, Bono. His and the band's commercial success internationally could mask their inner Irish reasons and compulsions. It's very easy to use abstractions, cloudy words like 'transcendence' about U2 without realizing how this Irish band instinctively understood those notions. Others would try to reproduce their passion, miss both their skill, dedication and context, and end up bellowing at the moon.

So it goes. As I finish this appraisal, U2 are beavering away in a Dublin studio, working on their next project. Almost twelve years ago, I breezed into a Dublin bar to meet some fresh-faced teenagers, drinking coke and lemonade. None of us ever believed it would come to *this*.

Bono: note his boots with the Cuban heels of which he was so fond that he had three pairs. In Dublin this style of boot became known as Bono boots

Liberty Hall – U2: the early benefit phase. This one was against Ireland's notorious anti-contraception laws, though the band were interrupted in mid-set while the women from the Contraception Action Campaign made their speeches. Still the gesture provokes thought about U2's early alleged puritan religious views. Later in '78, they headed a benefit for a short-lived 'Rock Against Sexism' group in Dublin's Magnet bar. Only fifty turned up, but those present thought it a dream date

The earliest
photograph of
the band, playing
support to Revolver,
McGonagle's 1978.

opposite right: The Edge
as early mop-top at
McGonagle's. To his
left, Irish rock's
redwood, the club's
famous plastic palm
tree

At the Project Arts Centre, 18 September 1978. The stage was always too small for them. Over Larry's head is a poster of Led Zeppelin, stamped 'Then Came The Virgin Prunes!'

opposite left: Bono, again, at the Project Arts Centre
Adam Clayton *right:* at work
above: Lounging in Trinity

Though ignorant of the blues or rock 'n' roll, both Bono and the Edge were investigating the principles of primitive recording long before they entered Sun studios. Both shots were taken in Trinity College where Dik's rooms functioned as a down-town office, coffee-house and occasional crash-pad for Lypton Village

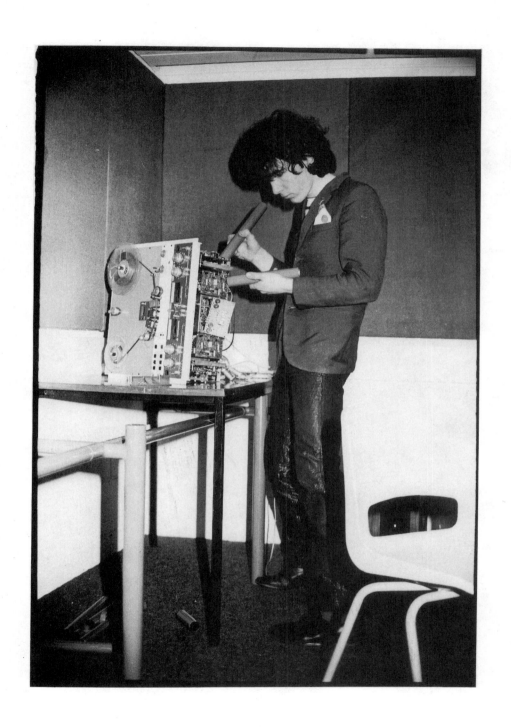

Bono's cigarette routine for 'Boy/Girl'. It had nothing to do with Roxy Music's 'Do The Strand'. Most times, Bono fumbled at the lighter or matchbox while the band launched a long instrumental break. In the future, he wouldn't even need this excuse to destroy their cues

After the Project Arts Centre gig in the
neighbouring Granary Bar, 18 September 1978

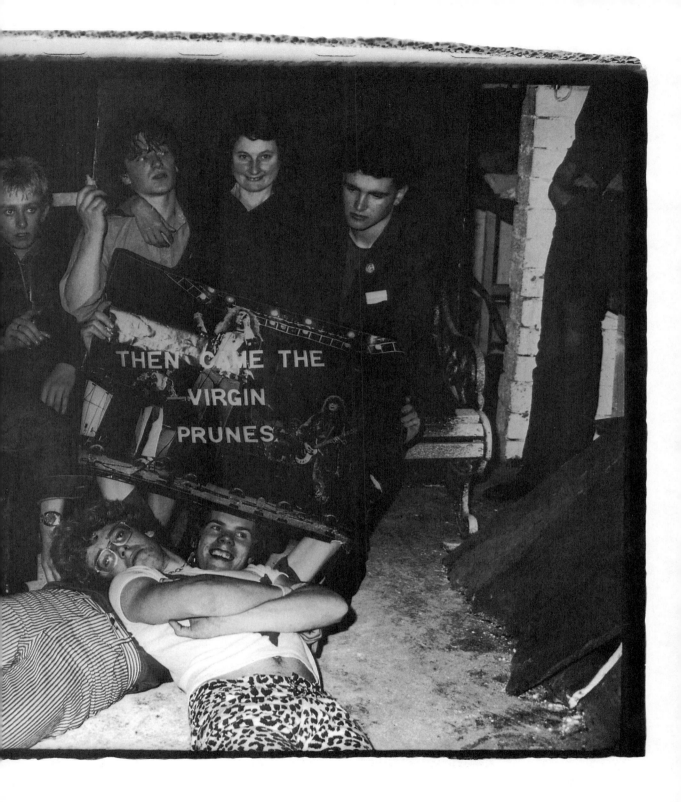

The consequences of Larry's day job. Guggi substitutes as U2 fake interview shots for the file and the Edge borrows Bono's jacket

Playing the Stardust as support to the Greedy Bastards, Phil Lynott's occasional combination of Thin Lizzy and Sex Pistols members. The only major venue on Dublin's Northside, the Stardust burnt down on 14 February 1981, causing the death of forty-eight young people

opposite right (bottom): Off-stage, behind Bono, Hugo McGuinness keeps his hand over the camera lens. Bewildered, he couldn't understand U2's Dublin reputation as they clattered and rattled away

above: Not so much the Unforgettable Fire and passion extinguisher as U2: the hardcore days!

opposite left: Bono and the Edge goofing again at Trinity. From their earliest days, U2 and especially Bono needed little encouragement to perform for the camera

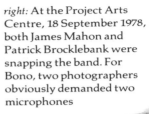

right: At the Project Arts Centre, 18 September 1978, both James Mahon and Patrick Brocklebank were snapping the band. For Bono, two photographers obviously demanded two microphones

Larry Mullen in triplicate and duffle-coat

Again at the Project Arts Centre. Note Adam's early leopard-spot mode

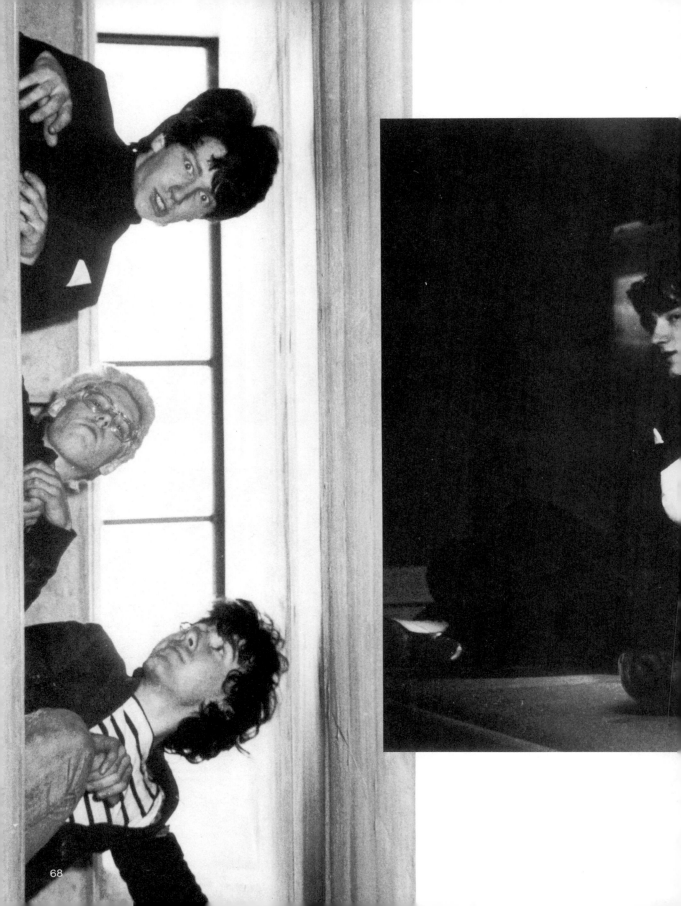

Again, without Larry, the threesome of Bono, Adam and the Edge posing in Trinity

Bono and Guggi play human extras, fronting Robert Ballagh's mural, *Three People and Jackson Pollock* in Trinity College Dublin. Blown up, the shot is now capable of an infinite regress

Adam further emphasizes U2's early interest in fire prevention

Peering over the Edge's right shoulder is Eric Briggs, roadie and, briefly, drumming understudy for Larry

Bono at the Crofton Airport hotel, late '78

It wasn't always U2 mania. Sometimes the shows
become rehearsals. Only six people turned up to the
Crofton Airport hotel. Three of them thought another
band was playing. Still, *top right*, Bono keeps smiling

above: Bono and U2 play the student Buttery bar in Trinity
opposite right: The Edge and Adam at the Jingle Balls
overleaf: The band at the Buttery with the Jingle Balls as background

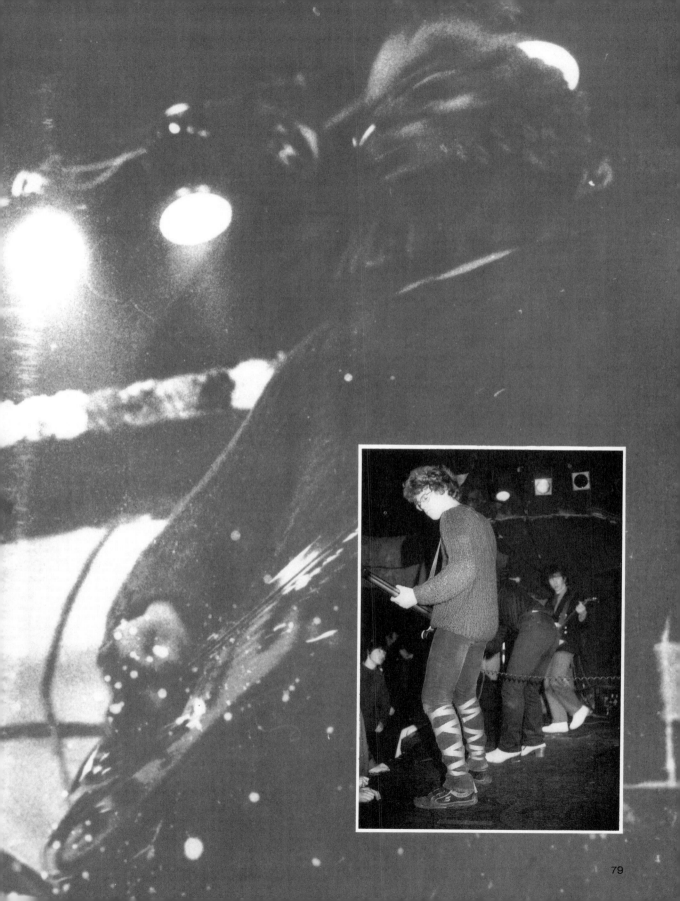

The Project Arts Centre was also a small theatre with props to tempt bands into more outlandish poses. As the Edge and Bono cradle toy guns, Adam proves he has no future ahead of him as a hat designer

preceding pages: Bono at the Jingle Balls and the Edge at the Top
Hat support to the Stranglers

above: Adam and Larry at the Project Arts Centre, supporting
Patrick Fitzgerald

opposite right: The Edge at Howth Youth Club, July '79

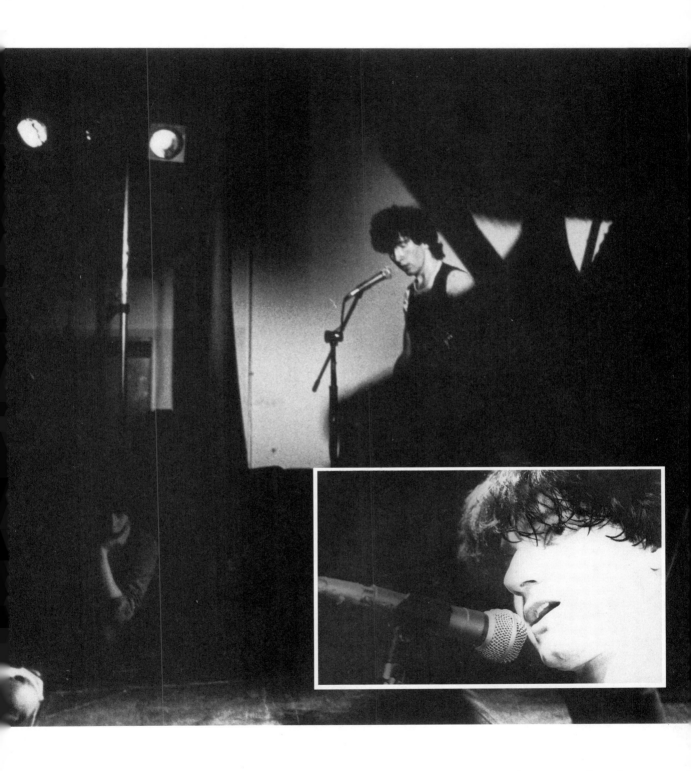

overleaf: U2 at McGonagle's

above: 'Waiting for the bus to come'. This was Bono's idea, according to Hugo; his notion of the surburban 'cartoon world' into which U2 were born

left: Early Hugo McGuinness publicity shots
Games – playing between the more serious posing

left to right: Elsie, Adam, Edge, Paul McGuinness, Bono, Aislinn's sister, Rachel O'Sullivan, girlfriend of Prunes bassist, Strongman (Trevor Rowan) and Larry. Loitering in the background: Guggi, Gavin Friday and Clive Rowan

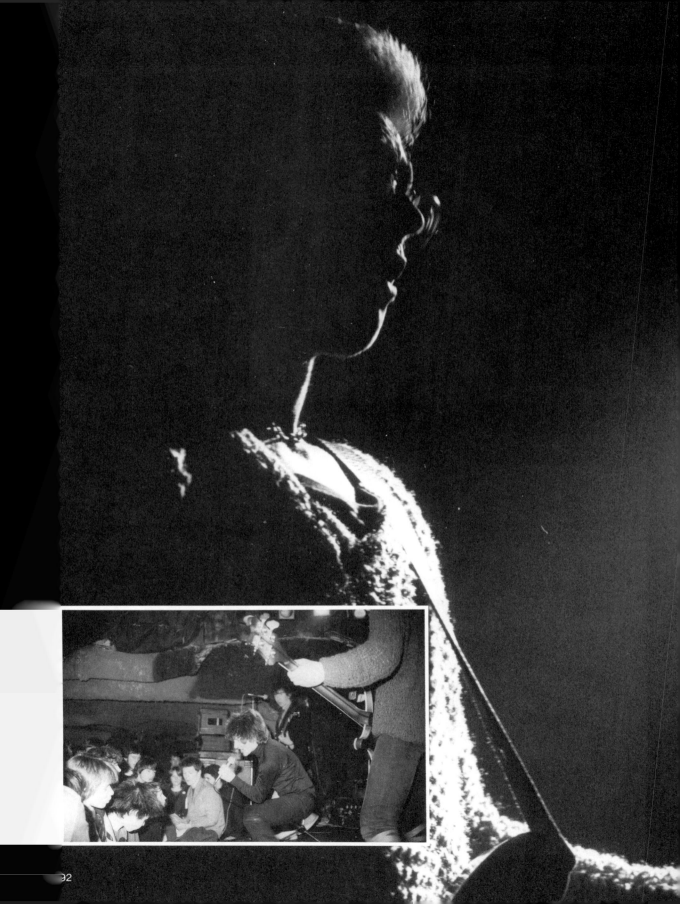

Summer 78: a Saturday afternoon matinee for the under-eighteens at McGonagle's

above: The Edge and Bono inspect the sleeve of 'U2:Three'

left: 'The Boy', Peter Rowan pummels a pensive Larry. The concept for the sleeve of U2's first album *Boy* was well thought out even before they had secured a record deal. Peter was already featured on the cover of their first single 'U2:Three'. When Hugo was shooting the session for the album sleeve, Peter got restless: 'Was this a big record, for a big record company?' he asked Hugo. 'Yes', the photographer replied. 'Then I'm worth more. Tell Bono, I'm going on strike,' Peter countered. As Bono negotiated extra payment of a box of Mars bars, Peter stood stock still with his arms behind his head, while Hugo snapped away. And so the cover was shot